HBR'S 10 MUST READS

On
Boards

HBR's 10 Must Reads series is the definitive collection of ideas and best practices for aspiring and experienced leaders alike. These books offer essential reading selected from the pages of *Harvard Business Review* on topics critical to the success of every manager.

Titles include:

On Boards

HARVARD BUSINESS REVIEW PRESS
Boston, Massachusetts

Copyright 2020 Harvard Business School Publishing Corporation

Library of Congress Cataloging-in-Publication Data is forthcoming.

ISBN: 978-1-63369-889-5
eISBN: 978-1-63369-890-1

The paper used in this publication meets the requirements of the American National Standard for Permanence of Paper for Publications and Documents in Libraries and Archives Z39.48-1992.

Contents

HBR'S 10 MUST READS

On
Boards

What Makes Great Boards Great

by Jeffrey A. Sonnenfeld

IN THE WAKE OF THE MELTDOWNS of such once great companies as Adelphia, Enron, Tyco, and WorldCom, enormous attention has been focused on the companies' boards. Were the directors asleep at the wheel? In cahoots with corrupt management teams? Simply incompetent? It seems inconceivable that business disasters of such magnitude could happen without gross or even criminal negligence on the part of board members. And yet a close examination of those boards reveals no broad pattern of incompetence or corruption. In fact, the boards followed most of the accepted standards for board operations: Members showed up for meetings; they had lots of personal money invested in the company; audit committees, compensation committees, and codes of ethics were in place; the boards weren't too small, too big, too old, or too young. Finally, while some companies have had problems with director independence because of the number of insiders on their boards, this was not true of all the failed boards, and board makeup was generally the same for companies with failed boards and those with well-managed ones.

In other words, they passed the tests that would normally be applied to ascertain whether a board of directors was likely to do a good job. And that's precisely what's so scary about these events. Viewing the breakdowns through the lens of my 25 years of experience studying board performance and CEO leadership leads me to one conclusion: It's time for some fundamentally new thinking about how corporate boards should operate and be evaluated. We need to consider not only how we structure the work of a board but also how we manage the social system a board actually is. We'll be fighting the wrong war if we simply tighten procedural rules for boards and ignore their more pressing need—to be strong, high-functioning work groups whose members trust and challenge one another and engage directly with senior managers on critical issues facing corporations.

The Inadequacy of Conventional Wisdom

Over time, good-governance advocates have developed no shortage of remedies for failures of governance. Most of these remedies are structural: They're concerned with rules, procedures, composition of committees, and the like, and together they're supposed to produce vigilant, involved boards. However, good and bad companies alike have already adopted most of those practices. Let's take a look at some of the most common.

Regular meeting attendance

Regular meeting attendance is considered a hallmark of the conscientious director. It matters a lot and, still, as shareholder activist Nell Minow comments, "Some big names on the boards . . . barely show up due to other commitments, and when they show, they're not prepared." Indeed, some WorldCom directors were on more than ten boards, so how well prepared could they be? *Fortune*'s 2001 list of the most-admired U.S. companies reveals no difference in the attendance records of board members of the most- and least-admired companies. Data from the Corporate Library, a corporate governance Web site and database cofounded by Minow, show the same "acceptable" attendance records at both kinds of companies. Good attendance is important for individual board members, but it alone doesn't seem to have much impact on whether companies are successful.

Idea in Brief

The meltdowns of once-great companies like Enron, Tyco, and WorldCom have riveted attention on their boards. Were the directors asleep at the wheel? In cahoots with corrupt management teams? Out-and-out criminals themselves?

None of the above. And that's what's so scary: Like most boards, those of the fallen giants followed all the rules. Members attended meetings regularly, had lots of personal money invested in the company, and weren't too old, young, or numerous. These boards even had audit committees, compensation committees, and ethics codes.

Yet great boards do far more than just follow good-governance rules. They're robust social systems: Their members know how to ferret out the truth, challenge one another, and even have a good fight now and then.

Equity involvement

Board members are assumed to be more vigilant if they hold big chunks of the company's stock—but data from the Corporate Library don't suggest that this measure by itself separates good boards from bad, either. Several members of the board of GE, *Fortune*'s most-admired corporation in 2001, had less than $100,000 of equity, whereas all board members of the least-admired companies held substantial equity stakes. Not only did all but one of the Enron board members own impressive amounts of equity in the company, but some were still buying as the shares collapsed.

Board member skills

Patrick McGurn of Institutional Shareholder Services, like other expert observers, has frequently questioned the financial literacy of troubled companies' audit committee members. It's certainly true that many board members have their jobs because they're famous, rich, well connected—anything but financially literate. But just as many board members have the training and smarts to detect problems and somehow fail to do their jobs anyway. At the time of their meltdowns, for example, Kmart had six current or recent *Fortune* 500 CEOs on its board, and Warnaco had several prominent financiers, a

Idea in Practice

To build better boards, CEOs, lead directors, and board members themselves can work to:

Create a Climate of Trust and Candor

If you're CEO, share important and difficult information with directors in time for them to digest it—not the night before a meeting. If you're a member, insist on *receiving* adequate information. To discourage members from creating back channels to line managers in pursuit of political agendas, give them access to company personnel and sites—then trust them not to meddle in day-to-day operations.

Foster Open Dissent

The willingness to challenge one another's assumptions and beliefs may be *the* most important characteristic of great boards—indicating bonds strong enough to withstand clashing viewpoints. Don't punish dissenters or forbid discussion of any subject. Probe silent board members for their opinions and the thinking behind their positions.

If you're asked to join a board, say no if you detect pressure to conform. Blind obedience puts your—and your company's—wealth and reputation at risk. An ideal board member, Home Depot chairman Bernie Marcus has said, "I don't think you want me on your board. I am contentious. I ask a lot of questions, and if I don't get the answers, I won't sit down."

well-known retail analyst, and a top-tier CEO; all those excellent credentials made little difference. On this measure, again, we find that *Fortune*'s most- and least-admired companies alike had board members with the training and experience to analyze complex financial issues and to understand what kinds of risks a company is taking on.

Despite Enron's disastrously complex financial schemes, no corporation could have had more appropriate financial competencies and experience on its board. The list includes a former Stanford dean who is an accounting professor, the former CEO of an insurance company, the former CEO of an international bank, a hedge fund manager, a prominent Asian financier, and an economist who is the former head of the U.S. government's Commodity Futures Trading Commission. Yet members of this board have claimed to have been confused by Enron's financial transactions.

Use a Fluid Portfolio of Roles

Don't let directors get trapped in typecast positions—the peacemaker, the damn-the-details big-picture person, the ruthless cost-cutter. Push everyone—including the CEO—to challenge his or her roles and assumptions. Require a big-picture person to dig deeply into the details of a particular business, or a peacemaker to play devil's advocate. Results? Wider views of the business and its available alternatives.

Ensure Individual Accountability

The most effective enforcement mechanism is peer pressure. Give directors tasks—for example, meeting with customers, suppliers, and distributors, or visiting plants or stores in the field—and require them to inform the rest of the board about the company's strategic and operational issues.

Evaluate Board Performance

No group's performance is assessed less rigorously than boards—yet no group learns without feedback. To conduct a full board review, a governance committee can evaluate the board's understanding and development of strategy, the quality of board meeting discussions, the level of candor and use of conflict, and the credibility of reports. It can evaluate individuals by examining initiative, preparation for and participation in discussions, and energy levels.

Board member age

According to one governance expert, "Enron melted down because it lacks independent directors and several are quite long in the tooth." His remarks reflect a general belief that boards become less effective as the average age of their members rises. My research on executives over the past two decades has shown that, to the contrary, age is often an asset, and this general finding is supported by board data from the Corporate Library. Charles Schwab, Cisco, and Home Depot all have had several board members who are well into their sixties. Michael Dell (Dell Computer placed tenth on *Fortune*'s 2001 list of most-admired companies) told me that when he incorporated in 1987, as a 21-year-old college dropout, he found it invaluable to have then 70-year-old George Kozmetsky, Teledyne's visionary founder and the former dean of the McCombs School of

Business in Austin, Texas, serve on the board; Kozmetsky stayed for more than a decade.

The past CEO's presence

The complicated reality is that sometimes a past CEO's presence is helpful and sometimes it's not. In the years I served on and even chaired commissions for the National Association of Corporate Directors (NACD), some commissioners regularly vilified the "old dragons" who haunted successors by serving on boards. In certain cases, this can be a problem; one can only imagine board meetings at Warnaco, where deposed CEO Linda Wachner voted her 9% of the company's equity for several months after her November 2001 termination. Alternately, a retired CEO can play an invaluable internal role as a mentor, sounding board, and link to critical outside parties. It's hard to imagine anyone arguing that Intel, Southwest Airlines, or Home Depot would be better off if their legendary retired CEOs Andy Grove, Herb Kelleher, or Bernie Marcus had just gone home to play golf.

Independence

Good-governance advocates and stock exchange heavyweights alike have argued that boards with too many insiders are less clean and less accountable. Some argue that Tyco's confusing spiral of acquisitions and the apparent self-dealing of the CEO at Adelphia Communications might have been less likely if their boards hadn't been dominated by insiders. Indeed, the New York Stock Exchange's Corporate Accountability and Standards Committee recently proposed requiring that the majority of a NYSE-listed corporation's directors be independent—this in response to the recent governance disasters. Governance reform proposals are also being developed by such business groups as the Conference Board and the Business Roundtable. Yet again, if you judge the most- and least-admired companies on *Fortune*'s 2001 list against this standard, no meaningful distinction emerges. Least-admired companies like LTV Steel, CKE Restaurants, Kmart, Warnaco, Trump Hotels and Casino Resorts, Federal-Mogul, and US Airways had only one or two inside directors on their boards; Enron had only two. By contrast, at various times in their histories, Home Depot had five insider directors on its 11-person board, Intel had three on a nine-person board, and Southwest Airlines had three on an eight-person board. Typically, half of Microsoft's board are insiders. Currently, three of Warren Buffett's seven Berkshire Hathaway board members have the Buffett name, and another is his long-term vice chairman.

United Parcel Service has ranked high on *Fortune*'s list of most-admired companies since the list was started, and half of the UPS management committee is on its board. Three outside board members have told me how well plugged-in they have felt over the years because the inside members are very candid and well informed. From what the outside directors have seen, none of the insiders has ever been afraid to debate a point with the boss, the CEO.

Board size and committees

A host of other issues that good-governance advocates propose turn out to be either not truly important or already in place at both good and bad companies. Take board size. Small's considered good, big's considered bad. But big boards exist at some great and admired companies— GE, Wal-Mart, and Schwab—along with some poorly performing companies like US Airways and AT&T. At the same time, small boards are part of the landscape at good companies like Berkshire Hathaway and Microsoft and some not-so-good companies like Trump.

Another area where good companies don't necessarily conform to the advice of good-governance advocates: executive sessions, which give boards the chance to evaluate their CEOs without interference. Executive sessions are also sometimes coupled with a designated lead director. But GE, the most-admired company in the country in 2001, didn't allow executive sessions in Jack Welch's day. Said Ken Langone, who serves on the boards of both GE and Home Depot, "Jack will give you all the time in the world to raise any issue you want, but he wants to be there during the discussion." GE's not alone; many good boards never have meetings that exclude the CEO.

Another supposed safeguard of good governance—audit and compensation committees—turns out to be near universal. A 2001 survey by the NACD and Institutional Shareholder Services of 5,000 public company boards shows that 99% have audit committees, and 91% have compensation committees. Sunbeam, Enron, Cendant, McKessonHBOC, and Waste Management all had the requisite number of committees and guidelines, yet accounting scandals still penetrated this governance shield. Let's not forget, either, that the audit committee at Enron was consulted about suspending the conflict-of-interest guidelines and willingly agreed to it.

The Importance of the Human Element

So if following good-governance regulatory recipes doesn't produce good boards, what does? The key isn't structural, it's social. The most involved, diligent, value-adding boards may or may not follow every recommendation in the good-governance handbook. What distinguishes exemplary boards is that they are robust, effective social systems. Let's see what that means.

A virtuous cycle of respect, trust, and candor

It's difficult to tease out the factors that make one group of people an effective team and another, equally talented group of people a dysfunctional one; well-functioning, successful teams usually have chemistry that can't be quantified. They seem to get into a virtuous cycle in which one good quality builds on another. Team members develop mutual respect; because they respect one another, they develop trust; because they trust one another, they share difficult information; because they all have the same, reasonably complete information, they can challenge one another's conclusions coherently; because a spirited give-and-take becomes the norm, they learn to adjust their own interpretations in response to intelligent questions.

The UPS board of directors has just that kind of chemistry, and as a result members have debated strategic decisions openly and constructively for years. The company's 1991 move from Connecticut to Georgia was hotly debated within the management committee, for example, but once the plan to move was agreed upon, the board chose a new location unanimously and never looked back. In the mid-1980s, after forging partnerships with delivery businesses around the world, a revolutionary concept at the time, the company decided to reverse course and become truly global itself. In just two years, UPS was running operations in more countries than are members of the United Nations. This strategic reversal is generally considered a brilliant move, one that might never have happened had board members not respected and trusted one another enough to consider that a smart move could be trumped by an even smarter one. The board even tolerated an open debate in 1992, led by a former CEO, over the company's widely recognized corporate color, brown—the hallmark of UPS's current advertising campaign.

A virtuous cycle of respect, trust, and candor can be broken at any point. One of the most common breaks occurs when the CEO doesn't trust the board enough to share information. What kind of CEO waits until the night before the board meeting to dump on the directors a phone-book-size report that includes, buried in a thicket of subclauses and footnotes, the news that earnings are off for the second consecutive quarter? Surely not a CEO who trusts his or her board. Yet this destructive, dangerous pattern happens all the time. Sometimes a CEO's lack of trust takes even more dramatic forms. It's stunning that Enron's chairman and CEO never told the board that whistle-blower Sherron Watkins had raised major questions about financial irregularities. It is impossible for a board to monitor performance and oversee a company if complete, timely information isn't available to the board.

It is, I should note, the responsibility of the board to insist that it receive adequate information. The degree to which this doesn't happen is astonishing. Consider Tyco. In recent quarters, it's suffered some of the worst strategic confusion I've ever witnessed: Seemingly every single public statement by the company's senior management has been contradicted by subsequent statements. For example, in January 2002, then CEO Dennis Kozlowski announced a plan to split the company into four pieces, only to reverse that plan a few months later. On a single day, senior managers announced first that a financial unit would be IPO'ed, next that it would be sold to an investment house, and finally that neither would occur. Where was the board? Why didn't directors demand a better accounting of the company's direction and well-being? What brought down the CEO eventually was an apparently private financial matter—the board seemed content to keep him on indefinitely.

Another sign that trust is lacking is when board members begin to develop back channels to line managers within the company. This can occur because the CEO hasn't provided sufficient, timely information, but it can also happen because board members are excessively political and are pursuing agendas they don't want the CEO to know about. If a board is healthy, the CEO provides sufficient information on time and trusts the board not to meddle in day-to-day operations. He or she also gives board members free access to people who can answer their questions, obviating the need for back channels.

Another common point of breakdown occurs when political factions develop on the board. Sometimes this happens because the CEO sees the board as an obstacle to be managed and encourages factions to develop, then plays them against one another. Pan Am founder Juan Trippe was famous for doing this. As early as 1939, the board forced him out of the CEO role, but he found ways to sufficiently terrorize the senior managers at the company and one group of board members that he was returned to office. When he was fired again following huge cost overruns on the Boeing 747 the company underwrote, he coerced the directors into naming a successor who was terminally ill.

Most CEOs aren't as manipulative as Trippe, and in fact, they're often frustrated by divisive, seemingly intractable cliques that develop on boards. Failing to neutralize such factions can be fatal. Several members of Jim Robinson's American Express board were willing to provide the advice, support, and linkage he needed—but the board was also riddled with complex political agendas. Eventually the visionary CEO was pushed out during a business downturn by a former chairman who wanted to reclaim the throne and a former top executive of another company who many felt simply missed the limelight.

The CEO, the chairman, and other board members can take steps to create a climate of respect, trust, and candor. First and most important, CEOs can build trust by distributing reports on time and sharing difficult information openly. In addition, they can break down factions by splitting up political allies when assigning members to activities such as site visits, external meetings, and research projects. It's also useful to poll individual board members occasionally: An anonymous survey can uncover whether factions are forming or if members are uncomfortable with an autocratic CEO or chairman. Other revelations may include board members' distrust of outside auditors, internal company reports, or management's competence. These polls can be administered by outside consultants, the lead director, or professional staff from the company.

A culture of open dissent

Perhaps the most important link in the virtuous cycle is the capacity to challenge one another's assumptions and beliefs. Respect and trust do not imply endless affability or absence of disagreement. Rather, they imply bonds among board members that are strong enough to withstand clashing viewpoints and challenging questions.

I'm always amazed at how common group-think is in corporate boardrooms. Directors are, almost without exception, intelligent, accomplished, and comfortable with power. But if you put them into a group that discourages dissent, they nearly always start to conform. The ones that don't often self-select out. Financier Ken Langone tells the story of a widely admired CEO who was invited to join the board of a famous corporation that is suffering great distress today. He was told that, as a matter of custom, new directors were expected to say nothing for the first 12 months. The candidate said, "Fine, I'll see you in a year," and of course never got the appointment. Langone explained that directors generally feel that they are under pressure to fit in so they'll be renominated. As he put it, "Almost no one wants to be a skunk at a lawn party."

Even a single dissenter can make a huge difference on a board. Bill George, a former CEO and chairman of the board of Medtronic, reported that a lone dissenter had forced his company to reconsider

Building an Effective Board

GOOD BOARD GOVERNANCE CAN'T BE LEGISLATED, but it can be built over time. Your best bets for success:

Create a Climate of Trust and Candor

Share important information with directors in time for them to read and digest it. Rotate board members through small groups and committees so they spend time together meeting key company personnel and inspecting company sites. Work to eliminate polarizing factions.

Foster a Culture of Open Dissent

If you're the CEO, don't punish mavericks or dissenters, even if they're sometime pains in the neck. Dissent is not the same thing as disloyalty. Use your own resistance as an opportunity to learn. Probe silent board members for their opinions, and ask them to justify their positions. If you're asked to join a board, say no if you detect pressure to conform to the majority. Leave a board if the CEO expects obedience. Otherwise, you put your wealth and reputation—as well as the assets and reputation of the company—at risk.

Utilize a Fluid Portfolio of Roles

Don't allow directors to get trapped in rigid, typecast positions. Ask them to develop alternative scenarios to evaluate strategic decisions, and push them to challenge their own roles and assumptions. Do the same thing yourself.

Ensure Individual Accountability

Give directors tasks that require them to inform the rest of the board about strategic and operational issues the company faces. This may involve collecting external data, meeting with customers, anonymously visiting plants and stores in the field, and cultivating links to outside parties critical to the company.

Evaluate the Board's Performance

Examine directors' confidence in the integrity of the enterprise, the quality of the discussions at the board meetings, the credibility of reports, the use of constructive professional conflict, the level of interpersonal cohesion, and the degree of knowledge. In evaluating individuals, go beyond reputations, résumés, and skills to look at initiative, roles and participation in discussions, and energy levels.

near unanimous decisions on several occasions. One pharmaceutical director held out in opposition to Medtronic's acquisition of Alza, a maker of drug delivery systems, saying it would take Medtronic into an area it knew nothing about. He was so convincing that the acquisition was abandoned, and in retrospect, that was the right decision. Another dissenter convinced George and the board to reverse themselves and not to get out of the angioplasty business—and, indeed, to intensify those services—and that shift has paid off handsomely.

Frequently, executive recruiters looking for leads during board candidate searches will ask, "Is this fellow a team player?" which is code for "Is this person compliant, or does he make trouble?" If a board member challenges major decisions, a company sometimes goes to great lengths to discredit the person. Consider Walter Hewlett—an academic; the cofounder's son, who controlled 18% of Hewlett-Packard stock; and someone with a deep understanding of the computer business—who had the temerity to question HP's proposed merger with Compaq in the fall of 2001. Despite the fact that technology mergers rarely work, his point of view was summarily dismissed internally. When he was forced to go public with his objections, he was ridiculed publicly in a smear campaign.

CEOs who don't welcome dissent try to pack the court, and the danger of that action is particularly clear right now. Recall that Enron board members Rebecca Mark and Clifford Baxter resigned reportedly because they were uncomfortable with paths the company had taken. And one can imagine a happier ending at Arthur Andersen had somebody said, "Wait a minute," when the document shredding began, or at Tyco when the board learned of millions in undisclosed loans to the CEO and didn't question them.

The CEO, the chairman, the lead director, and the board in general need to demonstrate through their actions that they understand the difference between dissent and disloyalty. This distinction cannot be legislated through nominating committee rules and guidelines for director résumés; it has to be something that leaders believe in and model. Home Depot chairman Bernie Marcus notes that, for one simple reason, he'd never serve on a board where dissent was discouraged: When he serves on a board, his reputation and his fortune are on the line. A lost reputation can't be regained, and director's insurance won't necessarily protect anyone's fortune, because there are always exemption clauses. Marcus has remarked, "I often say, 'I don't think you want me on your board. Because I am contentious. I ask a lot of questions and if I don't get the answers, I won't sit down.' That's the kind of board member that I want on my board . . . because our company needs help. We think we're bright, but we're not the smartest people in the world." Ken Langone corroborates this view of the Home Depot board. Both he and Marcus describe times when the board disagreed with management about strategic questions—when reformulating the small-store concept, for example, and when revisiting expansion into Latin America. The upshot wasn't that the board won and management lost, but rather that, after passionate disagreements had been voiced, together they arrived at new conclusions.

According to data complied by Kathleen Eisenhardt and L.J. Bourgeois, the highest-performing companies have extremely contentious boards that regard dissent as an obligation and that treat no subject as undiscussable. Directors at these companies scoff at some of the devices more timid companies use to encourage dissent, such as outside directors asking management to leave while they discuss company performance. What's the point of criticizing management, they ask, if management isn't there to answer the criticism? It should be noted that skepticism and dissent don't constitute disagreement for its own sake but rather are the by-products of a constantly evolving view of the business and of the world.

Fluid portfolio of roles

When board members don't challenge one another, individual directors' roles—the ruthless cost cutter, the damn-the-details big-picture guy, the split-the-differences peacemaker—can become stereotyped or rigid. Effective boards require their members to play a variety of roles, in some cases dipping deep into the details of a particular business, in others playing the devil's advocate, in still others serving as the project manager. Playing different roles gives directors a wider view of the business and of the alternatives available to it.

Occasionally board members can so thoroughly transcend their normal roles that they're able to change their minds about something they once built their lives around. This happened at PepsiCo in 1997 when the board decided to sell the various components of its well-run restaurant group. CEO Roger Enrico had previously turned around the unit—which had been the brainchild of two of Enrico's predecessors, Don Kendall and Wayne Calloway—and must have felt great pride of ownership. Yet he eventually convinced all that the restaurant unit should be sold so that it could flourish freely beyond the controls of the parent company. It's proved to be a brilliant decision.

Individual accountability

Board accountability is a tricky problem for CEOs, as a 2002 survey by the Yale School of Management and the Gallup Organization underscores. In that survey, fully 25% of CEOs claim that their board members do not appreciate the complexity of the businesses they oversee. In addition, we've all seen instances when individual responsibility dissolved in large groups. This certainly appears to have happened at Enron: Practically everyone involved has pointed the finger of blame at others or proclaimed his or her ignorance as a badge of honor. The fact that many board members were financially sophisticated seemed to have encouraged the other board members to defer to their expertise.

There are various methods for enforcing accountability. Home Depot's board members are expected to visit at least eight stores outside their home state between board meetings; GE's board members dine with the company's largest suppliers and distributors the night before the annual meeting. Perhaps the most effective enforcement mechanism, though, is old-fashioned peer pressure. Directors who take their duties seriously, and let their fellow directors know they're expected to do the same, are the best insurance against a board whose first question, upon receipt of the quarterly earnings report, is, "When's lunch?"

Performance evaluation

I can't think of a single work group whose performance gets assessed less rigorously than corporate boards. In 2001, the NACD surveyed 200 CEOs serving as outside directors of public firms. Sixty-three percent said those boards had never been subjected to a performance evaluation. Forty-two percent acknowledged that their own companies had never done a board evaluation. A 2001 Korn/Ferry study of board directors found that only 42% regularly assess board performance, and only 67% regularly evaluate the CEO.

This lack of feedback is self-destructive. Behavioral psychologists and organizational learning experts agree that people and organizations cannot learn without feedback. No matter how good a board is, it's bound to get better if it's reviewed intelligently.

A performance review can include a full board evaluation, individual directors' self-assessments, and directors' peer reviews of one another. Most often, the nominating or governance committee drives these evaluations. A full board review can include an evaluation of such dimensions as its understanding and development of strategy, its composition, its access to information, and its levels of candor and energy. In individual self-assessments, board members can review the use of their time, the appropriate use of their skills, their knowledge of the company and its industry, their awareness of key personnel, and their general level of preparation.

The peer review can consider the constructive and less constructive roles individual directors play in discussions, the value and use of various board members' skill sets, interpersonal styles, individuals' preparedness and availability, and directors' initiative and links to critical stakeholders. This process is often best driven by a board committee such as a nominating or governance committee, which is assigned the execution and follow-through responsibilities for this process.

Annual evaluations led PepsiCo and Target to change their processes for reviewing strategy with their boards. Instead of the mind-numbing, back-to-back, business-unit dog and pony shows that boards often suffer, each company decided to spend a full day of each board meeting looking in depth at the strategic challenges of a single business unit.

_____

We all owe the shareholder activists, accountants, lawyers, and analysts who study corporate governance a debt: In the 1980s and 1990s, they alerted us to the importance of independent directors, audit committees, ethical guidelines, and other structural elements that can help ensure that a corporate board does its job. Without a doubt, these good-governance guidelines have helped companies avoid problems, big and small. But they're not the whole story or even the longest chapter in the story. If a board is to truly fulfill its mission—to monitor performance, advise the CEO, and provide connections with a broader world—it must become a robust team—one whose members know how to ferret out the truth, challenge one another, and even have a good fight now and then.

Originally published in September 2002. Reprint R0209H

Building Better Boards

by David A. Nadler

IN BUSINESS, AS IN FAMILIES, overly permissive parenting is often blamed for egregious misbehavior. Recent scandals have exposed some boards as too passive, too indulgent, or flat-out oblivious to what goes on around them. As a result, companies facing new governance requirements are scrambling to buttress financial reporting, overhaul board structures—whatever it takes to become compliant. If they stop there, though, compliant is all they'll be. That would be a shame.

The key to better corporate governance lies in the working relationships between boards and managers, in the social dynamics of board interaction, and in the competence, integrity, and constructive involvement of individual directors. Patently, this is not the stuff of legislation. In fact, as others have noted ("What Makes Great Boards Great," Jeffrey A. Sonnenfeld, HBR, September 2002), many corporate scofflaws already had in place the "reforms" now prescribed as a vaccine against misconduct. Boards dissatisfied with lowest-common-denominator improvements cannot count on answers imposed from outside. Instead, they must think aspirationally and act practically, deciding where they want to go and then equipping themselves for the journey.

That journey will probably be a long one. Everyone knows what most boards have been: gentleman's-club-era relics characterized by ceremony and conformity. And everyone knows what boards should be: seats of challenge and inquiry that add value without meddling and make CEOs more effective but not all-powerful. A board can reach that destination only if it functions as a team, as we have come to understand teams over the past few decades.

The high-performance board, like the high-performance team, is competent, coordinated, collegial, and focused on an unambiguous goal. Such entities do not simply evolve; they must be constructed to an exacting blueprint. At Mercer Delta, we call that act "board building."

The challenge of board building is huge; most companies don't know where to begin. To help them, we've developed an agenda and a set of tools that boards can use to define and achieve their objectives. The following guidance derives from our recent work with the CEOs and directors of more than two dozen major companies on the topics of board effectiveness, governance reforms, and CEO performance appraisal and succession.

We also collaborated with the Center for Effective Organizations at the University of Southern California in Los Angeles to survey more than 300 chiefly independent directors representing the boards of more than 200 large corporations. In general, the results of our survey mirrored our firsthand observations. One point that emerged repeatedly was the importance of regular self-assessment when building a strong board.

The Right Mind-Set

Board building is an ongoing activity, a process of continuous improvement, which means boards must keep coming back to the same questions about purpose, resources, and effectiveness. The best mechanisms for doing that are annual self-assessments. According to our survey, conducting and acting on such assessments are among the top activities most likely to improve board performance overall.

Of course, not everyone does what they know is best for them. Only 56% of respondents to our survey said their boards' performance is formally evaluated on a regular basis. And only one-quarter of those—or 16% of the entire sample—have a plan to address the concerns raised by their assessments. Clearly, many boards lack data from which to draw conclusions about their success and processes for using the data they do have to improve.

But to assess or not to assess isn't really the question: The New York Stock Exchange now requires annual board evaluations. Companies

Idea in Brief

Companies facing new requirements for governance are scrambling to buttress financial-reporting systems, overhaul board structures—whatever it takes to comply. But there are limits to how much good governance can be imposed from the outside.

Boards know what they ought to be: seats of challenge and inquiry that add value without meddling and make CEOs more effective but not all-powerful. A board can reach that goal only if it functions as a high-performance team, one that is competent, coordinated, collegial, and focused on an unambiguous goal. Such entities don't just evolve; they must be constructed to an exacting blueprint—what the author calls board building. In this article, Nadler offers an agenda and a set of tools that boards can use to define and achieve their objectives.

It's important for a board to conduct regular self-assessments and to pay attention to the results of those analyses. As a first step, the directors and the CEO should agree on which of the following common board models best fits the company: passive, certifying, engaged, intervening, or operating. The directors and the CEO should then analyze which business tasks are most important and allot sufficient time and resources to them. Next, the board should take inventory of each director's strengths to ensure that the group as a whole possesses the skills necessary to do its work. Directors must exert more influence over meeting agendas and make sure they have the right information at the right time and in the right format to perform their duties. Finally, the board needs to foster an engaged culture characterized by candor and a willingness to challenge.

An ambitious board-building process, devised and endorsed both by directors and by management, can potentially turn a good board into a great one.

do retain great flexibility around what to assess and how, as well as how to apply the results. Some boards skate by with paper-and-pencil surveys comprising recycled checklists cobbled together by another company's attorneys. That will keep them listed, but it won't do much to improve their minimalist approach to governance.

Others treat self-assessment as a transformational exercise. The boards of Medtronic, Service Corporation International, Bank of Montreal, and Best Western, among others, have self-assessed themselves into high-performance teams, rethinking members' roles and working relationships. Such extensive reinvention requires serious time and energy—scarce commodities for directors and CEOs. Self-assessment is no cursory glance in the mirror but rather an exhaustive culling of quantitative and qualitative data through surveys, confidential interviews, and facilitated group discussions.

The investment is worth it. By making routine the practice of rigorous introspection, boards ensure that they are fit to cope with existing circumstances and adapt to new ones.

The Right Role

Like most quests for change, board building begins with a vision. Specifically, boards must decide how engaged they want to be in influencing management's decisions and the company's direction. With this step, they move beyond the letter of reform and begin to focus on its spirit. We have identified five board types that fall along a continuum from least to most involved. (See the exhibit "How engaged should we be?") At the start of any board-building program, the directors and the CEO should agree among themselves which of the following models best fits the company.

The passive board
This is the traditional model. The board's activity and participation are minimal and at the CEO's discretion. The board has limited accountability. Its main job is ratifying management's decisions.

The certifying board
This model emphasizes credibility to shareholders and the importance of outside directors. The board certifies that the business is managed properly and that the CEO meets the board's requirements. It also oversees an orderly succession process.

The engaged board
In this model, the board serves as the CEO's partner. It provides insight, advice, and support on key decisions. It recognizes its

How engaged should we be?

At the start of any board-building program, the directors and the CEO need to agree what their level of involvement will be. The following are five possible board models, which fall along a continuum from least to most involved.

Least involved —— Most involved

The passive board	The certifying board	The engaged board	The intervening board	The operating board
Functions at the discretion of the CEO.	Certifies to shareholders that the CEO is doing what the board expects and that management will take corrective action when needed.	Provides insight, advice, and support to the CEO and management team.	Becomes intensely involved in decision making around key issues.	Makes key decisions that management then implements.
Limits its activities and participation.		Recognizes its ultimate responsibility to oversee CEO and company performance; guides and judges the CEO.	Convenes frequent, intense meetings, often on short notice.	Fills gaps in management experience.
Limits its accountability.	Emphasizes the need for independent directors and meets without the CEO.	Conducts useful, two-way discussions about key decisions facing the company.		
Ratifies management's preferences.	Stays informed about current performance and designates external board members to evaluate the CEO.	Seeks out sufficient industry and financial expertise to add value to decisions.		
	Establishes an orderly succession process.	Takes time to define the roles and behaviors required by the board and the boundaries of CEO and board responsibilities.		
	Is willing to change management to be credible to shareholders.			

responsibility for overseeing CEO and company performance. The board conducts substantive discussions of key issues and actively defines its role and boundaries.

The intervening board

This model is common in a crisis. The board becomes deeply involved in making key decisions about the company and holds frequent, intense meetings.

The operating board

This is the deepest level of ongoing board involvement. The board makes key decisions that management then implements. This model is common in early-stage start-ups whose top executives may have specialized expertise but lack broad management experience.

The point of this exercise isn't to pack boards into rigid boxes. These characterizations are, after all, essentially archetypes. Real-world boards slide back and forth across the scale, their levels of engagement changing as issues and circumstances do. A passive or certifying board in crisis, for instance, may morph temporarily into an intervening board to remove the CEO, and then into an operating board until a new leader is in place.

Still, selecting a level of engagement provides the philosophical framework for everything that follows. Simply having that conversation is a significant first step toward improved board performance. The board may find that it disagrees sharply with the executive team about its role; or that individual directors harbor divergent views, making it difficult to act in concert. Having characterized itself to itself and to management, the board can evaluate each subsequent decision for fidelity to the model.

The Right Work

Establishing an overarching level of engagement helps board directors set expectations and ground rules for their roles relative to senior managers' roles. But an engagement philosophy—like most expressions of general principle—does not apply equally to all spheres of activity. Boards, after all, potentially participate in dozens of distinct areas.

Many board tasks are familiar legal obligations: approving mergers and acquisitions; providing counsel to senior management; hiring, firing, and setting compensation; evaluating the CEO; ensuring effective audit procedures; monitoring investments; and so on. The latest governance requirements call upon boards to spell out those duties in written charters. At the end of each year, they go down the checklist and affirm, "Yes, we did that." But that is a recipe for compliance, not necessarily for good governance. A better approach is to translate these mandates into categories of work, each composed of several activities.

Using a form like the one shown in the exhibit "Which tasks are most important?" directors can rate the existing and optimal levels of engagement for each activity on a sliding scale. Activities that are chiefly management's responsibility receive a one; activities that fall exclusively within the purview of the board get a five. Senior managers should fill out the same form.

The results provide fodder for two forms of gap analysis. First, by comparing actual and desirable levels of engagement for each activity, the board can plot in great detail where to pump up or down its energies. Second, juxtaposing directors' and managers' views of the board's role may surface disagreements that otherwise act like submerged mines. Occasionally, the reverse happens: The directors at one large media company we worked with, for example, were pleasantly surprised when managers rated the board's optimal involvement in some areas higher than the board had rated itself.

This exercise has other applications as well. As the directors are considering all the scenarios that might require changes in involvement, they're forced to contemplate the future. The board can also use this form to track how well it is fulfilling its self-defined mission and whether meetings devote the right amount of time to the right topics. Finally, it is a starting point to determine whether directors possess adequate skills, experience, and knowledge in the areas that matter most.

Which tasks are most important?

Using a form like the one shown here, board directors and management can rate the existing and optimal levels of board engagement for each strategic business activity on a scale of one to five. (One represents areas that are chiefly management's responsibility, and five represents areas that are exclusively the board's responsibility.) This exercise may surface gaps between where the board needs to be focused and where it is actually spending its time and resources.

Sample:

	Current engagement						Desired engagement						The gap
	1	2	3	4	5	?	1	2	3	4	5	?	
1. Strategic direction	①	2	3	4	5	?	1	2	3	④	5	?	3
2. Strategic plans	①	2	3	4	5	?	1	2	3	4	⑤	?	4
3. Strategy implementation	1	②	3	4	5	?	1	2	③	4	5	?	1

higher number denotes area to work on

1	No engagement
2	Low engagement
3	Moderate engagement
4	High engagement
5	Exclusive engagement
?	Not applicable/don't know

Strategy

	Current engagement						Desired engagement						The gap
	1	2	3	4	5	?	1	2	3	4	5	?	
1. Strategic direction	1	2	3	4	5	?	1	2	3	4	5	?	
2. Strategic plans	1	2	3	4	5	?	1	2	3	4	5	?	
3. Strategy implementation	1	2	3	4	5	?	1	2	3	4	5	?	

Strategic transactions

	Current engagement						Desired engagement						The gap
4. Major investments	1	2	3	4	5	?	1	2	3	4	5	?	
5. Portfolio change (M&A)	1	2	3	4	5	?	1	2	3	4	5	?	

Operations	Current engagement						Desired engagement						The gap
6. R&D	1	2	3	4	5	?	1	2	3	4	5	?	
7. Manufacturing	1	2	3	4	5	?	1	2	3	4	5	?	
8. Marketing and sales	1	2	3	4	5	?	1	2	3	4	5	?	
9. IT	1	2	3	4	5	?	1	2	3	4	5	?	
Human resources and organization													
10. Leadership development	1	2	3	4	5	?	1	2	3	4	5	?	
11. Non-CEO executive compensation	1	2	3	4	5	?	1	2	3	4	5	?	
12. Human capital	1	2	3	4	5	?	1	2	3	4	5	?	
13. Organization	1	2	3	4	5	?	1	2	3	4	5	?	
14. Corporate culture	1	2	3	4	5	?	1	2	3	4	5	?	
Financial management													
15. Financial strategy	1	2	3	4	5	?	1	2	3	4	5	?	
16. Capital structure	1	2	3	4	5	?	1	2	3	4	5	?	
17. Liquidity management	1	2	3	4	5	?	1	2	3	4	5	?	
18. Dividend policy	1	2	3	4	5	?	1	2	3	4	5	?	
19. Financial reporting	1	2	3	4	5	?	1	2	3	4	5	?	

(continued)

Which tasks are most important? (continued)

	Current engagement						Desired engagement						The gap
Risk management													
20. Enterprise risk management	1	2	3	4	5	?	1	2	3	4	5	?	
21. Ethical performance and compliance	1	2	3	4	5	?	1	2	3	4	5	?	
22. Audit	1	2	3	4	5	?	1	2	3	4	5	?	
External relations													
23. Brand positioning and integrity	1	2	3	4	5	?	1	2	3	4	5	?	
24. Shareholder relations	1	2	3	4	5	?	1	2	3	4	5	?	
25. Legal and regulatory	1	2	3	4	5	?	1	2	3	4	5	?	
26. Other constituencies	1	2	3	4	5	?	1	2	3	4	5	?	
CEO effectiveness													
27. CEO performance appraisal	1	2	3	4	5	?	1	2	3	4	5	?	
28. CEO compensation	1	2	3	4	5	?	1	2	3	4	5	?	
29. CEO succession	1	2	3	4	5	?	1	2	3	4	5	?	
Corporate governance													
30. Board effectiveness	1	2	3	4	5	?	1	2	3	4	5	?	
31. Director selection	1	2	3	4	5	?	1	2	3	4	5	?	
32. Director assessment	1	2	3	4	5	?	1	2	3	4	5	?	
Other (please specify)													
33.	1	2	3	4	5	?	1	2	3	4	5	?	

The Right People

A team is only as good as its members, and high-quality board members are alarmingly scarce. Eighty-one percent of our survey respondents said it's become more difficult to recruit qualified directors; close to 40% said their boards lack an effective process for selecting new members.

In addition, reform efforts unduly emphasize several narrow aspects of board composition. Sarbanes-Oxley prescribes a heavy dose of independent directors, but the real issue isn't independence; it's competence. We are not referring merely to the technical expertise of audit committee members but to all competencies related to the company, its environment, and its industry.

Composition assessments look at both the collective capabilities of the board and the attributes of each director. Again, our survey is revealing. More than 90% of respondents said their boards possess the collective capabilities to be effective. By comparison, directors' individual proficiencies inspired less confidence. Only:

- 73% of respondents said their colleagues have detailed knowledge of the company's industry;

- 69% said their colleagues have accounting and public-reporting expertise;

- 61% said their colleagues understand the company's key technologies and business practices;

- 60% said their colleagues possess expertise in global business issues;

- 58% said their colleagues contribute potentially valuable external contacts.

The work-categories exercise described earlier is the cornerstone of composition assessment. Boards take inventory of each director's strengths—based on professional experience and technical knowledge—and align them with activities that require maximum board involvement. The resulting capabilities profile illustrates the match—sometimes the alarming mismatch—between what the board needs and what directors can actually do. Such knowledge is critical for producing director recruitment profiles.

Continental Airlines, for example, was determined to enlist the best directors possible to help fight the battles engulfing its industry. The board thoroughly analyzed the company's business issues to determine what skills and experience it needed. Directors zeroed in on knowledge of the airline and travel industries, an understanding of marketing and consumer behavior, access to key business and political contacts, and experience with industry reconfiguration.

The board then defined the capabilities and qualities expected of all directors, such as independence, business credibility, financial expertise, confidence, and teamwork. To be as representative as possible, it took into account directors' knowledge of geographic markets—particularly their knowledge of key Continental hubs— CEO experience, leadership in the business sectors, and gender and ethnic diversity.

Next, the board assessed all of its directors and mapped their skills, experience, and backgrounds against the new criteria. The gaps became fodder for hypertargeted recruitment profiles. In the end, several board members voluntarily stepped down to make way for new directors who had the capabilities Continental needed to compete successfully.

Capabilities profiles also provide a safe mechanism for directors and senior managers to broach sensitive subjects. "For about a year, I'd wanted to raise the issue of recruiting more directors with industry experience," said the CEO of a *Fortune* 500 company involved in a massive turnaround. "I felt sure this issue would make several board members defensive, so I held off." Then the board performed a composition assessment. "To my surprise, they raised this issue themselves," the CEO told us, "and tasked the nominating committee to develop a list of board candidates with exactly the kind of experience I felt we needed—all without my having to be the heavy."

Evaluating personal performance, of course, requires precision and delicacy. It is not surprising that 76% of our survey respondents report that the boards on which they sit conduct no individual assessments. Under growing pressure to perform, however, boards must recognize which directors need help, which should not be nominated for another term, and which should be cut loose. Consequently, more boards are adopting formal assessments of individual directors, including peer review.

The peer review at one multinational financial services company illustrates how such assessments work. It comprises 18 questions rating individual members' demonstrated knowledge of key areas, their understanding of and preparation for their roles as directors, the quality of their input or advice, and their contributions to board interaction. All board members, including the member being evaluated, fill out the form. (The exhibit "What are our members' strengths and weaknesses?" compares the ratings one director gave himself with the ratings others gave him.) The company furnishes such reports to each board member and to the board's independent chairman, who uses them to guide discussion during directors' annual reviews. Peer feedback has influenced decisions about recruitment, retirement, committee leadership and selection, and education initiatives for directors.

The Right Agenda

Agenda management is a mundane-sounding subject if ever there was one. Agendas, however, dictate what the board discusses and at what length. To control the agenda is to control the work of the board.

Historically, management has been in control. Nearly 60% of our survey respondents said they can't influence their own agendas. The result has been decades of choreographed ceremonies substituting for meetings where real work gets done. At many companies, directors routinely endure a parade of precisely scripted presentations, occasionally followed by perfunctory discussion and the inevitable vote to ratify management's recommendations. CEOs, if so inclined, can overload the agenda with so many show-and-tell segments that they crowd out serious questions, troublesome concerns, or authentic debate.

"At many U.S. companies, the board meetings are shorter, and there's much less discussion," says one retired CEO who has sat on

What are our members' strengths and weaknesses?

Use of peer-review tools is becoming more common among boards interested in formally assessing their individual directors. In the example here, the performance of one director at a multinational financial services company was rated on a scale of one (lowest performance) to five (highest performance) in four areas: contributions to board interaction; knowledge of key areas; understanding of director's role; and quality of input at meetings. His peers generally gave him more credit for his knowledge than the director gave himself. But when the subject was interaction, the director's peers perceived him as undermining board deliberations by talking too much, listening too little, and squelching constructive debate. Meanwhile, the director clearly considered listening and engaging to be among his strong suits.

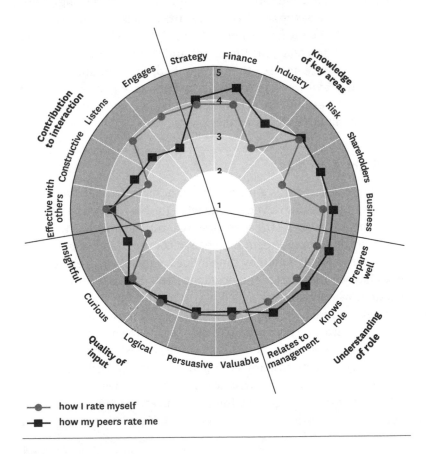

----●---- how I rate myself

----■---- how my peers rate me

the boards of both U.S. and European companies. "It's more, 'Bang, bang, here's a nice presentation on interesting issues.' It's like going to a diner for a meal. If you don't finish your food fast, they will take it away from you."

But with the call to accountability, corporate boards can no longer doze behind the wheel while management steers. To the extent that CEOs participate in the board-building process (and CEOs *must* participate in the board-building process) they acquiesce to some level of power sharing—a high level in the engaged, intervening, and operating models. The presiding director can collaborate with the CEO to devise an agenda agreeable to both. Alternatively, at the end of each board meeting, participants can collectively set the agenda for the next one. In any case, the rating of tasks (which, you'll recall, has been blessed by both the board *and* management) is the touchstone. Directors and managers can review the agendas and minutes of meetings past to ascertain how much time they devote to each area. They then compare those findings with the board's priorities to establish a correlation between interest bestowed and time spent.

The board at Target, a corporate governance leader, has gone further, transforming agenda management into something of an art. At the start of each year, the board sets three top priorities—for example, strategic direction, capital allocation, and succession planning. It then places each topic at the top of the agenda for at least one upcoming meeting. Target's board also devotes one meeting a year to setting the strategic direction for each major operating division, an acknowledgement of the company's growing complexity. Directors never stint on questions and debate, requiring management to submit major items for board approval at least one meeting prior to the scheduled vote so they have the chance to discuss them. But they are chary of their time and insist that presentations be short and to the point.

Boards should find ways to stay engaged with the company's issues outside of regular meetings as well. Even without managerial diversions, board meetings are simply too packed with must-accomplish items to allow an in-depth examination of any one. That is frustrating for directors who want to dig deeper into the meatiest subjects, most notably succession planning and strategy. Annual off-site meetings or retreats, one-on-one conclaves involving CEOs and directors, and sit-downs between groups of directors and employees who have common interests all make the intervals between meetings fruitful.

The board's standing committees can also provide continuity. In response to the heightened focus on accounting and financial reporting, for example, many audit committees now meet—in person or via teleconferencing—more often than the board as a whole. Certainly, committees give directors the chance to concentrate on specific issues, developing deeper expertise in the process. But in general, boards have come to rely less and less on committees, motivated in part by the concern that some will emerge with greater influence than others and impair directors' ability to work together.

The Right Information

The corporate secretary of a major company explained to us the "dark side" of communications between senior management and the board. "There are two equally effective ways of keeping a board in the dark," he said. "One is to provide them with too little information. The other, ironically, is to provide too much." The secretary went on to describe his own experience on the board of a public corporation: "We received reams of financial information in advance of each board meeting, which was way too much to absorb and could not be properly understood without considerable background information."

Thus do boards fall prey to the confusion of data with information, which is no less real a problem for being a cliché. Too many board directors are overwhelmed by fat stacks of often insignificant numbers but lack the right information presented in the right way to produce informed action. We're constantly surprised—though perhaps we shouldn't be—when directors who have served on boards for years confess that they don't really understand how their companies make money.

Certainly, boards face a huge information challenge. Directors are outsiders with limited time to learn about the company. If knowledge is power, then the balance lies with managers, who live and breathe operations. Indeed, only 28% of the directors in our survey said they have independent channels for obtaining useful information about the company. The rest rely on what management chooses to share with them. Throughout our research, directors asked us repeatedly, "How can I tell what's really going on?"

In some cases, a little class time helps correct the imbalance. One company we worked with, for example, decided that its board lacked the background to intelligently review its strategy, business model, and performance. So the CFO walked audit committee members through the company's balance sheet line by line and later did the same for the entire board in an intensive three-hour workshop. Directors, including some who had been on the board for years, came away with a much better understanding of important issues.

In that case, the board diagnosed its own problem. Other boards, however, suffer from a more general discomfort: the feeling that something is missing or preventing them from doing their jobs. Often, that something is a particular kind of information. The board of Axcan Pharma, for example, conducted a self-assessment that exposed concern about the conflation of chairman and CEO roles. Further conversations narrowed the focus: Directors, it turned out, worried less about the conflation of roles than about a lack of information regarding acquisitions the CEO was pursuing. The solution was to change the information flow to the board rather than separate the two roles. Similarly, at Best Western, directors expressed dissatisfaction about the board's role in strategic direction. Their chief complaint? They weren't getting information on risks and returns before being asked to ratify major initiatives.

Such knowledge malnutrition is common. Boards often subsist on just two sources of information. The first is retrospective data on corporate performance and operations—in other words, trailing indicators. The second is presentations by management—particularly by the CEO, whose articulation of a vision and interpretation of financials significantly shape boards' views. Given those meager rations, it's no wonder companies get into deep trouble before their boards find out.

Not long ago, we worked with a board that was under sharp criticism for taking too long to remove a CEO following major performance shortfalls and spectacular valuation declines. But the directors shouldn't have been faulted for dragging their feet. As one explained, "Six months ago, we had a very articulate CEO who made a very eloquent case about the company, and we had financial measures that indicated we were one of the most valuable market capitalization companies in the country. How were we to know what was going on below? In fact, once we saw the problems, we acted with blinding speed, although in many ways it was too late."

It is management's responsibility to ensure that boards get the right information at the right time and in the right format to perform their duties. The best boards design processes to deliver formal information that combines both leading and lagging performance indicators, which will vary by industry and company. But boards should also be free to collect information on their own, informally and without management supervision. Directors at General Electric and Target, for example, are required to periodically visit company facilities unaccompanied by senior executives.

The Right Culture

Against a backdrop of governance progress, many boards appear positively antediluvian. The boardroom is dark and richly paneled. A plaque engraved with a member's name adorns each chair. No one argues passionately about anything. Robert's Rules of Order prevail.

Those are just some visible artifacts of traditional board culture—a huge obstacle to directors seeking greater engagement. Culture is a system of informal, unwritten, yet powerful norms derived from shared values that influence behavior. We know that culture affects teams: Even those doing the same work with identical structures and similar composition perform differently depending on their social systems and beliefs. Thus, passive boards, governed as they are by formality and reserve, will perform differently from boards like the one described in the sidebar "Do We Have an Engaged Culture?" Engaged cultures are characterized by candor and a willingness to

Do We Have an Engaged Culture?

ENGAGED CULTURES ARE CHARACTERIZED by candor and a willingness to challenge. In each of the following areas, engaged boards reflect the social and work dynamics of a high-performance team.

Agendas

- The agendas limit presentation time and maximize discussion time.
- There is lots of opportunity for informal interaction among directors.

Norms

- Board members are honest yet constructive.
- Board members are ready to ask questions and willing to challenge leadership.
- Board members actively seek out other directors' views and contributions.
- Board members spend appropriate time on important issues.

Beliefs

"If I don't come prepared, I will be embarrassed."

"If I don't actively participate, I won't be fulfilling my responsibility."

"I'll earn the respect of my fellow directors by making valuable contributions and taking responsibility for what we do together."

"If I can't carry my load, or if I can't agree with what's going on, I should resign."

Values

- The board serves the business community by actively participating in governance.
- The board is responsible to the company's various stakeholders and constituencies.
- Board members are personally accountable for what goes on in the company.
- The board is responsible for maintaining the company's stature in the industry.
- Board members respect one another.

challenge, and they reflect the social and work dynamics of a high-performance team.

Structures, composition, information flow—these things can be designed. Culture, by contrast, develops over time and tends to reward those who perpetuate it, making it difficult to change. At one financial institution in the midst of a self-assessment, some directors argued for a more open and participatory culture. But the majority clung to the status quo. Proponents of change recognized that as long as the board's composition stayed the same, the old culture wasn't going anywhere.

Boards cannot easily change their cultures. But as members start to act as a team, board cultures will change. The closer directors get to an engaged culture, the closer they are to being the best boards possible.

Although governance reform is, strictly speaking, an imposition, boards should view it as a catalyst. Yes, it is far harder to clean house than to simply tidy up, but the rewards are proportionately greater. An ambitious board-building process, devised and endorsed by directors and management, can turn a good board into a great one. But that transformation happens only when boards define their optimal roles and tasks and marshal the people, agendas, information, and culture to support them.

At its most effective, board building contributes not only to performance but also to member satisfaction. "I've served on this board for nearly ten years, and this is the first time I've really sat down and thought about how we have been working together," said the director of a consumer products company engaged in such a project. "Our discussions always focus on how we are addressing everything on the overloaded agenda. Now that I've spent some time thinking about this, there are definitely some things we could do better.

"It also made me think about why I joined this board in the first place," he said. "Somewhere between all the meetings and the calls, I seem to have lost sight of that."

Originally published in May 2004. Reprint R0405G

The Error at the Heart of Corporate Leadership

by Joseph L. Bower and Lynn S. Paine

IN THE FALL OF 2014, the hedge fund activist and Allergan shareholder Bill Ackman became increasingly frustrated with Allergan's board of directors. In a letter to the board, he took the directors to task for their failure to do (in his words) "what you are paid $400,000 per year to do on behalf of the Company's owners." The board's alleged failure: refusing to negotiate with Valeant Pharmaceuticals about its unsolicited bid to take over Allergan—a bid that Ackman himself had helped engineer in a novel alliance between a hedge fund and a would-be acquirer. In presentations promoting the deal, Ackman praised Valeant for its shareholder-friendly capital allocation, its shareholder-aligned executive compensation, and its avoidance of risky early-stage research. Using the same approach at Allergan, he told analysts, would create significant value for its shareholders. He cited Valeant's plan to cut Allergan's research budget by 90% as "really the opportunity." Valeant CEO Mike Pearson assured analysts that "all we care about is shareholder value."

These events illustrate a way of thinking about the governance and management of companies that is now pervasive in the financial community and much of the business world. It centers on the idea that management's objective is, or should be, maximizing value for shareholders, but it addresses a wide range of topics—from performance measurement and executive compensation to share-holder rights, the role of directors, and corporate responsibility. This thought system has been embraced not only by hedge fund activists like Ackman but also by institutional investors more generally, along with many boards, managers, lawyers, academics, and even some regulators and lawmakers. Indeed, its precepts have come to be widely regarded as a model for "good governance" and for the brand of investor activism illustrated by the Allergan story.

Yet the idea that corporate managers should make maximizing shareholder value their goal—and that boards should ensure that they do—is relatively recent. It is rooted in what's known as agency theory, which was put forth by academic economists in the 1970s. At the theory's core is the assertion that shareholders own the corporation and, by virtue of their status as owners, have ultimate authority over its business and may legitimately demand that its activities be conducted in accordance with their wishes.

Attributing ownership of the corporation to shareholders sounds natural enough, but a closer look reveals that it is legally confused and, perhaps more important, involves a challenging problem of accountability. Keep in mind that shareholders have no legal duty to protect or serve the companies whose shares they own and are shielded by the doctrine of limited liability from legal responsibility for those companies' debts and misdeeds. Moreover, they may generally buy and sell shares without restriction and are required to disclose their identities only in certain circumstances. In addition, they tend to be physically and psychologically distant from the activities of the companies they invest in. That is to say, public company shareholders have few incentives to consider, and are not generally viewed as responsible for, the effects of the actions they favor on the corporation, other parties, or society more broadly. Agency theory has yet to grapple with the implications of the accountability vacuum that results from accepting its central—and in our view, faulty—premise that shareholders own the corporation.

The effects of this omission are troubling. We are concerned that the agency-based model of governance and management is being practiced in ways that are weakening companies and—if applied

Idea in Brief

The Problem

A widespread belief holds that "maximizing shareholder value" is the number one responsibility of boards and managers. But that's confused as a matter of corporate law and a poor guide for managerial behavior—and it has a huge accountability problem baked into it.

The Solution

A company's health—not its shareholders' wealth—should be the primary concern of those who manage corporations. That may sound like a small change, but it could make companies less vulnerable to damaging forms of activist investing—and make it easier for managers to focus on the long term.

even more widely, as experts predict—could be damaging to the broader economy. In particular we are concerned about the effects on corporate strategy and resource allocation. Over the past few decades the agency model has provided the rationale for a variety of changes in governance and management practices that, taken together, have increased the power and influence of certain types of shareholders over other types and further elevated the claims of shareholders over those of other important constituencies—without establishing any corresponding responsibility or accountability on the part of shareholders who exercise that power. As a result, managers are under increasing pressure to deliver ever faster and more predictable returns and to curtail riskier investments aimed at meeting future needs and finding creative solutions to the problems facing people around the world.

Don't misunderstand: We are capitalists to the core. We believe that widespread participation in the economy through the ownership of stock in publicly traded companies is important to the social fabric, and that strong protections for shareholders are essential. But the health of the economic system depends on getting the role of shareholders right. The agency model's extreme version of shareholder centricity is flawed in its assumptions, confused as a matter of law, and damaging in practice. A better model would recognize the critical role of shareholders but also take seriously the idea that corporations are independent entities serving multiple purposes and endowed by law with the potential to endure over time. And it would acknowledge accepted legal principles holding that directors and managers have duties to the corporation as well as to shareholders. In other words, a better model would be more company centered.

Before considering an alternative, let's take a closer look at the agency-based model.

Foundations of the Model

The ideas underlying the agency-based model can be found in Milton Friedman's well-known *New York Times Magazine* article of 1970 denouncing corporate "social responsibility" as a socialist doctrine. Friedman takes shareholders' ownership of the corporation as a given. He asserts that "the manager is the agent of the individuals who own the corporation" and, further, that the manager's primary "responsibility is to conduct the business in accordance with [the owners'] desires." He characterizes the executive as "an agent serving the interests of his principal."

These ideas were further developed in the 1976 *Journal of Financial Economics* article "Theory of the Firm," by Michael Jensen and William Meckling, who set forth the theory's basic premises:

- Shareholders own the corporation and are "principals" with original authority to manage the corporation's business and affairs.

- Managers are delegated decision-making authority by the corporation's shareholders and are thus "agents" of the shareholders.

- As agents of the shareholders, managers are obliged to conduct the corporation's business in accordance with shareholders' desires.

- Shareholders want business to be conducted in a way that maximizes their own economic returns. (The assumption that shareholders are unanimous in this objective is implicit throughout the article.)

Jensen and Meckling do not discuss shareholders' wishes regarding the ethical standards that managers should observe in conducting the business, but Friedman offers two views in his *Times* article. First he writes that shareholders generally want managers "to make as much money as possible while conforming to the basic rules of the society, both those embodied in law and those embodied in ethical custom." Later he suggests that shareholders simply want managers to use resources and pursue profit by engaging "in open and free competition without deception or fraud." Jensen and Meckling agree with Friedman that companies should not engage in acts of "social responsibility."

Much of the academic work on agency theory in the decades since has focused on ensuring that managers seek to maximize shareholder returns—primarily by aligning their interests with those of shareholders. These ideas have been further developed into a theory of organization whereby managers can (and should) instill concern for shareholders' interests throughout a company by properly delegating "decision rights" and creating appropriate incentives. They have also given rise to a view of boards of directors as an organizational mechanism for controlling what's known as "agency costs"—the costs to shareholders associated with delegating authority to managers. Hence the notion that a board's principal role is (or should be) monitoring management, and that boards should design executive compensation to align management's interests with those of shareholders.

The Model's Flaws

Let's look at where these ideas go astray.

1. Agency theory is at odds with corporate law: Legally, shareholders do not have the rights of "owners" of the corporation, and managers are not shareholders' "agents."

As other scholars and commentators have noted, the idea that shareholders own the corporation is at best confusing and at worst incorrect. From a legal perspective, shareholders are beneficiaries of the corporation's activities, but they do not have "dominion" over a piece of property. Nor do they enjoy access to the corporate premises or use of the corporation's assets. What shareholders do own is their shares. That generally gives them various rights and privileges, including the right to sell their shares and to vote on certain matters, such as the election of directors, amendments to the corporate charter, and the sale of substantially all the corporation's assets.

Furthermore, under the law in Delaware—legal home to more than half the *Fortune* 500 and the benchmark for corporate law—the right to manage the business and affairs of the corporation is vested in a board of directors elected by the shareholders; the board delegates that authority to corporate managers.

Within this legal framework, managers and directors are fiduciaries rather than agents—and not just for shareholders but also for the corporation. The difference is important. Agents are obliged to carry out the wishes of a principal, whereas a fiduciary's obligation is to exercise independent judgment on behalf of a beneficiary. Put differently, an agent is an order taker, whereas a fiduciary is expected to make discretionary decisions. Legally, directors have a fiduciary duty to act in the best interests of the corporation, which is very different from simply doing the bidding of shareholders.

2. The theory is out of step with ordinary usage: Shareholders are not owners of the corporation in any traditional sense of the term, nor do they have owners' traditional incentives to exercise care in managing it.

This observation is even truer today than when it was famously made by Adolf Berle and Gardiner Means in their landmark 1932 study *The Modern Corporation and Private Property.* Some 70% of shares in U.S.-listed companies today are held by mutual funds, pension funds, insurance companies, sovereign funds, and other institutional investors, which manage them on behalf of beneficiaries such as households, pensioners, policy holders, and governments. In many instances the beneficiaries are anonymous to the company whose shares the institutions hold. The professionals who manage these investments are typically judged and rewarded each quarter on the basis of returns from the total basket of investments managed. A consequence is high turnover in shares (seen in the exhibit "Average holding period for public company shares"), which also results from high-frequency trading by speculators.

The decisions of asset managers and speculators arise from expectations regarding share price over a relatively short period of time. As the economy passes through cycles, the shares of companies in entire industry sectors move in and out of favor. Although the shareholders of record at any given moment may vote on an issue brought before them, they need not know or care about the company whose shares they hold. Moreover, the fact that they can hedge or immediately sell their shares and avoid exposure to the longer-term effects

Average holding period for public company shares

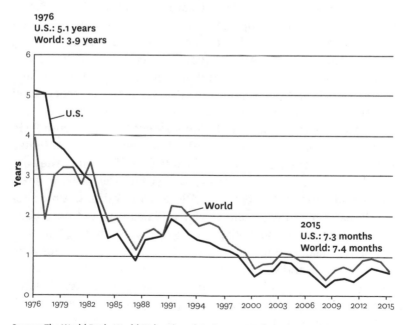

1976
U.S.: 5.1 years
World: 3.9 years

U.S.

World

2015
U.S.: 7.3 months
World: 7.4 months

Years

Source: The World Bank, World Federation of Exchanges Database.

of that vote makes it difficult to regard them as proprietors of the company in any customary sense.

The anonymity afforded the shares' beneficial owners further attenuates their relationship to the companies whose shares they own. Some 85% of publicly traded shares in the United States are held in the name of an institution serving as an intermediary—the so-called street name—on behalf of itself or its customers. And of the ultimate owners of those shares, an estimated 75% have instructed their intermediaries not to divulge their identities to the issuing company.

3. The theory is rife with moral hazard: Shareholders are not accountable as owners for the company's activities, nor do they have the responsibilities that officers and directors do to protect the company's interests.

The problem with treating shareholders as proprietors is exacerbated by the absence of another traditional feature of ownership: responsibility for the property owned and accountability—even legal liability, in some cases—for injuries to third parties resulting from how that property is used. Shareholders bear no such responsibility. Under the doctrine of limited liability, they cannot be held personally liable for the corporation's debts or for corporate acts and omissions that result in injury to others.

With a few exceptions, shareholders are entitled to act entirely in their own interest within the bounds of the securities laws. Unlike directors, who are expected to refrain from self-dealing, they are free to act on both sides of a transaction in which they have an interest. Consider the contest between Allergan and Valeant. A member of Allergan's board who held shares in Valeant would have been expected to refrain from voting on the deal or promoting Valeant's bid. But Allergan shareholders with a stake in both companies were free to buy, sell, and vote as they saw fit, with no obligation to act in the best interests of either company. Institutional investors holding shares in thousands of companies regularly act on deals in which they have significant interests on both sides.

In a well-ordered economy, rights and responsibilities go together. Giving shareholders the rights of ownership while exempting them from the responsibilities opens the door to opportunism, overreach, and misuse of corporate assets. The risk is less worrying when shareholders do not seek to influence major corporate decisions, but it is acute when they do. The problem is clearest when temporary holders of large blocks of shares intervene to reconstitute a company's board, change its management, or restructure its finances in an effort to drive up its share price, only to sell out and move on to another target without ever having to answer for their intervention's impact on the company or other parties.

4. The theory's doctrine of alignment spreads moral hazard throughout a company and narrows management's field of vision.
Just as freedom from accountability has a tendency to make shareholders indifferent to broader and longer-term considerations, so agency theory's recommended alignment between managers' interests and those of shareholders can skew the perspective of the entire organization. When the interests of successive layers of management are "aligned" in this manner, the corporation may become so biased toward the narrow interests of its current shareholders that it fails to meet the requirements of its customers or other constituencies. In extreme cases it may tilt so far that it can no longer function effectively. The story of Enron's collapse reveals how thoroughly the body of a company can be infected.

The notion that managing for the good of the company is the same as managing for the good of the stock is best understood as a theoretical conceit necessitated by the mathematical models that many economists favor. In practical terms there is (or can be) a stark difference. Once Allergan's management shifted its focus from sustaining long-term growth to getting the company's stock price to $180 a share—the target at which institutional investors were willing to hold their shares—its priorities changed accordingly. Research was cut, investments were eliminated, and employees were dismissed.

5. The theory's assumption of shareholder uniformity is contrary to fact: Shareholders do not all have the same objectives and cannot be treated as a single "owner."

Agency theory assumes that all shareholders want the company to be run in a way that maximizes their own economic return. This simplifying assumption is useful for certain purposes, but it masks important differences. Shareholders have differing investment objectives, attitudes toward risk, and time horizons. Pension funds may seek current income and preservation of capital. Endowments may seek long-term growth. Young investors may accept considerably more risk than their elders will tolerate. Proxy voting records indicate that shareholders are divided on many of the resolutions put before them. They may also view strategic opportunities differently. In the months after Valeant announced its bid, Allergan officials met with a broad swath of institutional investors. According to Allergan's lead independent director, Michael Gallagher, "The diversity of opinion was as wide as could possibly be"—from those who opposed the deal and absolutely did not want Valeant shares (the offer included both stock and cash) to those who saw it as the opportunity of a lifetime and could not understand why Allergan did not sit down with Valeant immediately.

The Agency-Based Model in Practice

Despite these problems, agency theory has attracted a wide following. Its tenets have provided the intellectual rationale for a variety of changes in practice that, taken together, have enhanced the power of shareholders and given rise to a model of governance and management that is unrelenting in its shareholder centricity. Here are just a few of the arenas in which the theory's influence can be seen:

Executive compensation

Agency theory ideas were instrumental in the shift from a largely cash-based system to one that relies predominantly on equity. Proponents of the shift argued that equity-based pay would better align the interests of executives with those of shareholders. The same argument was used to garner support for linking pay more closely to stock performance and for tax incentives to encourage such "pay for performance" arrangements. Following this logic, Congress adopted legislation in 1992 making executive pay above $1 million deductible only if it is "performance based." Today some 62% of executive pay is in the form of equity, compared with 19% in 1980.

Disclosure of executive pay

Agency theory's definition of performance and its doctrine of alignment undergird rules proposed by the SEC in 2015 requiring companies to expand the information on executive pay and shareholder returns provided in their annual proxy statements. The proposed rules call for companies to report their annual total shareholder return (TSR) over time, along with annual TSR figures for their peer group, and to describe the relationships between their TSR and their executive compensation and between their TSR and the TSR of their peers.

Shareholders' rights

The idea that shareholders are owners has been central to the push to give them more say in the nomination and election of directors and to make it easier for them to call a special meeting, act by written consent, or remove a director. Data from FactSet and other sources indicates that the proportion of S&P 500 companies with majority voting for directors increased from about 16% in 2006 to 88% in 2015; the proportion with special meeting provisions rose from 41% in 2002 to 61% in 2015; and the proportion giving shareholders proxy access rights increased from less than half a percent in 2013 to some 39% by mid-2016.

The power of boards

Agency thinking has also propelled efforts to eliminate staggered boards in favor of annual election for all directors and to eliminate "poison pills" that would enable boards to slow down or prevent "owners" from voting on a premium offer for the company. From 2002 to 2015, the share of S&P 500 companies with staggered boards dropped from 61% to 10%, and the share with a standing poison pill fell from 60% to 4%. (Companies without a standing pill may still adopt a pill in response to an unsolicited offer—as was done by the Allergan board in response to Valeant's bid.)

Management attitudes

Agency theory's conception of management responsibility has been widely adopted. In 1997 the Business Roundtable issued a statement declaring that "the paramount duty of management and of boards of directors is to the corporation's stockholders" and that "the principal objective of a business enterprise is to generate economic returns to its owners." Issued in response to pressure from institutional investors, the statement in effect revised the Roundtable's earlier position that "the shareholder must receive a good return but the legitimate concerns of other constituencies also must have the appropriate attention." Various studies suggest ways in which managers have become more responsive to shareholders. Research indicates, for instance, that companies with majority (rather than plurality) voting for directors are more apt to adopt shareholder proposals that garner majority support, and that many chief financial officers are willing to forgo investments in projects expected to be profitable in the longer term in order to meet analysts' quarterly earnings estimates. According to surveys by the Aspen Institute, many business school graduates regard maximizing shareholder value as their top responsibility.

Investor behavior

Agency theory ideas have facilitated a rise in investor activism and legitimized the playbook of hedge funds that mobilize capital for the express purpose of buying company shares and using their position as "owners" to effect changes aimed at creating shareholder value. (The sidebar "The Activist's Playbook" illustrates how agency theory ideas have been put into practice.) These investors are intervening more frequently and reshaping how companies allocate resources. In the process they are reshaping the strategic context in which all companies and their boards make decisions.

The Activist's Playbook

FOR AN UNDERSTANDING of the agency-based model in practice, there is no better place to look than an activist campaign. As a first step, the activist acquires shares in the targeted company—typically somewhere between 5% and 10%, but sometimes less than 1%. Shares in hand, he then claims the right to issue directives. (To leverage that power, he will often alert other hedge funds to his actions.) The language of ownership typically plays a prominent role. For example, in 2014, to advance a takeover of Allergan by Valeant Pharmaceuticals, Bill Ackman, of Pershing Square Capital Management, attacked Allergan's board for failing to do what the directors were paid to do "on behalf of the Company's owners." The activist may challenge the board's professionalism by appealing to agency theory norms of directorship. In one letter to the Allergan board, Ackman declared: "Your actions have wasted corporate resources, delayed enormous potential value creation for shareholders, and are professionally and personally embarrassing for you."

Although campaigns differ in their particulars, the activist's playbook for increasing shareholder value is fairly standard. As our colleagues Ian Gow and Suraj Srinivasan (with others) have documented in their study of nearly 800 campaigns at U.S. companies from 2004 to 2012, activists tend to focus on capital structure, strategy, and governance. They typically call for some combination of cutting costs, adding debt, buying back shares, issuing special dividends, spinning off businesses, reconstituting the board, replacing the CEO, changing the strategy, and selling the company or its main asset. Tax reduction is another element of many activist programs.

An activist whose demands go unheeded may initiate a proxy fight in an attempt to replace incumbent board members with directors more willing to do the activist's bidding. In a few instances, activists have even offered their chosen nominees special bonuses to stand for election or additional incentives for increasing shareholder value in their role as directors.

By most indications, hedge fund activists have been quite successful in effecting the changes they've sought. As reported by the industry, more companies are being targeted—473 worldwide in the first half of 2016 (including 306 in the United States), up from 136 worldwide in all of 2010—and activists' demands are frequently being met. In the United States in 2015, 69% of demands were at least partially satisfied, the highest proportion since 2010. Activists are also gaining clout in the boardroom, where they won 397 seats at U.S. companies in 2014 and 2015. Although activist hedge funds saw outflows of some $7.4 billion in the first three quarters of 2016, assets under management were estimated at more than $116 billion in late 2016, up from $2.7 billion in 2000.

Taken individually, a change such as majority voting for directors may have merit. As a group, however, these changes have helped create an environment in which managers are under increasing pressure to deliver short-term financial results, and boards are being urged to "think like activists."

Implications for Companies

To appreciate the strategic implications of a typical activist program, it is instructive to use a tool developed in the 1960s by the Boston Consulting Group to guide the resource-allocation process. Called the growth share matrix, the tool helped managers see their company as a portfolio of businesses with differing characteristics. One group of businesses might be mature and require investment only for purposes of modest expansion and incremental improvement. Assuming they have strong market share relative to their nearest competitors, those businesses are likely to be profitable and generate cash. Another group might also have leading positions but be in fast-growing markets; they, too, are profitable, but they require heavy investment to maintain or improve market share. A third group might have weak competitive positions in mature markets; these businesses require cash for survival but have no prospects for growth or increased profits. A final group might be in rapidly growing new markets where several companies are competitive and prospects are bright but risky.

The developers of the matrix called these four groups cash cows, stars, dogs, and bright prospects, respectively. The segmentation was meant to ensure that cash cows were maintained, stars fully funded, dogs pruned, and a limited number of bright prospects chosen for their longer-term potential to become stars. (See the exhibit "The growth share matrix.") When companies don't manage a portfolio in this holistic fashion, funds tend to get spread evenly across businesses on the basis of individual projects' forecasted returns.

It's a simple tool—but using it well is not simple at all. Managing a cash cow so that it remains healthy, nurturing star businesses in the face of emerging competition, fixing or divesting unpromising

The growth share matrix

BCG's growth share matrix enables companies to manage a portfolio of businesses: "cash cows," mature businesses that throw off cash; fast-growing "stars"; businesses with a weak position and few prospects for growth ("dogs"); and risky but big-upside businesses in fast-growing markets ("bright prospects").

Source: Boston Consulting Group.

businesses, and selecting one or two bright prospects to grow—all this takes talented executives who can function effectively as a team. Companies that succeed in managing this ongoing resource-allocation challenge can grow and reinvent themselves continually over time.

The growth share matrix illuminates the strategic choices managers face as they seek to create value indefinitely into the future. It's also useful for showing how to drive up a company's share price in the short term. Suppose a corporation were to sell off the dogs, defund the bright prospects, and cut expenses such as marketing and R&D from the stars. That's a recipe for dramatically increased earnings, which would, in turn, drive up the share price. But the corporation might lose bright prospects that could have been developed into the stars and cash cows of the future.

The activist investor Nelson Peltz's 2014 proposal for DuPont provides an example of this idea. At the core of his three-year plan for increasing returns to shareholders was splitting the company into three autonomous businesses and eliminating its central research function. One of the new companies, "GrowthCo," was to consist of DuPont's agriculture, nutrition and health, and industrial biosciences businesses. A second, "CyclicalCo/CashCo," was to include the low-growth but highly cash-generative performance materials, safety, and electronics businesses. The third was the performance chemicals unit, Chemours, which DuPont had already decided to spin off. In growth-share-matrix terms, Peltz's plan was, in essence, to break up DuPont into a cash cow, a star, and a dog—and to eliminate some number of the bright prospects that might have been developed from innovations produced by centralized research. Peltz also proposed cutting other "excess" costs, adding debt, adopting a more shareholder-friendly policy for distributing cash from CyclicalCo/CashCo, prioritizing high returns on invested capital for initiatives at GrowthCo, and introducing more shareholder-friendly governance, including tighter alignment between executive compensation and returns to shareholders. The plan would effectively dismantle DuPont and cap its future in return for an anticipated doubling in share price.

Value Creation or Value Transfer?

The question of whether shareholders benefit from such activism beyond an initial bump in stock price is likely to remain unresolved, given the methodological problems plaguing studies on the subject. No doubt in some cases activists have played a useful role in waking up a sleepy board or driving a long-overdue change in strategy or management. However, it is important to note that much of what activists call value creation is more accurately described as value transfer. When cash is paid out to shareholders rather than used to fund research, launch new ventures, or grow existing businesses, value has not been created. Nothing has been created. Rather, cash that would have been invested to generate future returns is simply being paid out to current shareholders. The lag time between when such decisions are taken and when their effect on earnings is evident exceeds the time frames of standard financial models, so the potential for damage to the company and future shareholders, not to mention society more broadly, can easily go unnoticed.

Given how long it takes to see the fruits of any significant research effort (Apple's latest iPhone chip was eight years in the making), the risk to research and innovation from activists who force deep cuts to drive up the share price and then sell out before the pipeline dries up is obvious. It doesn't help that financial models and capital markets are notoriously poor at valuing innovation. After Allergan was put into play by the offer from Valeant and Ackman's Pershing Square Capital Management, the company's share price rose by 30% as other hedge funds bought the stock. Some institutions sold to reap the immediate gain, and Allergan's management was soon facing pressure from the remaining institutions to accelerate cash flow and "bring earnings forward." In an attempt to hold on to those shareholders, the company made deeper cuts in the workforce than previously planned and curtailed early-stage research programs. Academic studies have found that a significant proportion of hedge fund interventions involve large increases in leverage and large decreases in investment, particularly in research and development.

The activists' claim of value creation is further clouded by indications that some of the value purportedly created for shareholders is actually value transferred from other parties or from the general public. Large-sample research on this question is limited, but one study suggests that the positive abnormal returns associated with the announcement of a hedge fund intervention are, in part, a transfer of wealth from workers to shareholders. The study found that workers' hours decreased and their wages stagnated in the three years after an intervention. Other studies have found that some of the gains for shareholders come at the expense of bondholders. Still other academic work links aggressive pay-for-stock-performance arrangements to various misdeeds involving harm to consumers, damage to the environment, and irregularities in accounting and financial reporting.

We are not aware of any studies that examine the total impact of hedge fund interventions on all stakeholders or society at large. Still, it appears self-evident that shareholders' gains are sometimes simply transfers from the public purse, such as when management improves earnings by shifting a company's tax domicile to a lower-tax jurisdiction—a move often favored by activists, and one of Valeant's proposals for Allergan. Similarly, budget cuts that eliminate exploratory research aimed at addressing some of society's most vexing challenges may enhance current earnings but at a cost to society as well as to the company's prospects for the future.

Hedge fund activism points to some of the risks inherent in giving too much power to unaccountable "owners." As our analysis of agency theory's premises suggests, the problem of moral hazard is real—and the consequences are serious. Yet practitioners continue to embrace the theory's doctrines; regulators continue to embed them in policy; boards and managers are under increasing pressure to deliver short-term returns; and legal experts forecast that the trend toward greater shareholder empowerment will persist. To us, the prospect that public companies will be run even more strictly according to the agency-based model is alarming. Rigid adherence to the model by companies uniformly across the economy could easily result in even more pressure for current earnings, less investment in R&D and in people, fewer transformational strategies and innovative business models, and further wealth flowing to sophisticated investors at the expense of ordinary investors and everyone else.

Toward a Company-Centered Model

A better model, we submit, would have at its core the health of the enterprise rather than near-term returns to its shareholders. Such a model would start by recognizing that corporations are independent entities endowed by law with the potential for indefinite life. With the right leadership, they can be managed to serve markets and society over long periods of time. Agency theory largely ignores these distinctive and socially valuable features of the corporation, and the associated challenges of managing for the long term, on the grounds that corporations are "legal fictions." In their seminal 1976 article, Jensen and Meckling warn against "falling into the trap" of asking what a company's objective should be or whether the company has a social responsibility. Such questions, they argue, mistakenly imply that a corporation is an "individual" rather than merely a convenient legal construct. In a similar vein, Friedman asserts that it cannot have responsibilities because it is an "artificial person."

In fact, of course, corporations *are* legal constructs, but that in no way makes them artificial. They are economic and social organisms whose creation is authorized by governments to accomplish objectives that cannot be achieved by more-limited organizational forms such as partnerships and proprietorships. Their nearly 400-year history of development speaks to the important role they play in society. Originally a corporation's objectives were set in its charter—build and operate a canal, for example—but eventually the form became generic so that corporations could be used to accomplish a wide variety of objectives chosen by their management and governing bodies. As their scale and scope grew, so did their power. The choices made by corporate decision makers today can transform societies and touch the lives of millions, if not billions, of people across the globe.

The model we envision would acknowledge the realities of managing these organizations over time and would be responsive to the needs of all shareholders—not just those who are most vocal at a given moment. Here we offer eight propositions that together provide a radically different and, we believe, more realistic foundation for corporate governance and shareholder engagement.

1. Corporations are complex organizations whose effective functioning depends on talented leaders and managers.

The success of a leader has more to do with intrinsic motivation, skills, capabilities, and character than with whether his or her pay is tied to shareholder returns. If leaders are poorly equipped for the job, giving them more "skin in the game" will not improve the situation and may even make it worse. (Part of the problem with equity-based pay is that it conflates executive skill and luck.) The challenges of corporate leadership—crafting strategy, building a strong organization, developing and motivating talented executives, and allocating resources among the corporation's various businesses for present and future returns—are significant. In focusing on incentives as the key to ensuring effective leadership, agency theory diminishes these challenges and the importance of developing individuals who can meet them.

2. Corporations can prosper over the long term only if they're able to learn, adapt, and regularly transform themselves.

In some industries today, companies may need reinvention every five years to keep up with changes in markets, competition, or technology. Changes of this sort, already difficult, are made more so by the idea that management is about assigning individuals fixed decision rights, giving them clear goals, offering them incentives to achieve those goals, and then paying them (or not) depending on whether the goals are met. This approach presupposes a degree of predictability, hierarchy, and task independence that is rare in today's organizations. Most tasks involve cooperation across organizational lines, making it difficult to establish clear links between individual contributions and specific outcomes.

3. Corporations perform many functions in society.

One of them is providing investment opportunities and generating wealth, but corporations also produce goods and services, provide employment, develop technologies, pay taxes, and make other contributions to the communities in which they operate. Singling out any one of these as "the purpose of the corporation" may say more about the commentator than about the corporation. Agency economists, it seems, gravitate toward maximizing shareholder wealth as the central purpose. Marketers tend to favor serving customers. Engineers lean toward innovation and excellence in product performance. From a societal perspective, the most important feature of the corporation may be that it performs all these functions simultaneously over time. As a historical matter, the original purpose of the corporation—reflected in debates about limited liability and general incorporation statutes—was to facilitate economic growth by enabling projects that required large-scale, long-term investment.

4. Corporations have differing objectives and differing strategies for achieving them.

The purpose of the (generic) corporation from a societal perspective is not the same as the purpose of a (particular) corporation as seen by its founders, managers, or governing authorities. Just as the purposes and strategies of individual companies vary widely, so must their performance measures. Moreover, companies' strategies are almost always in transition as markets change. An overemphasis on TSR for assessing and comparing corporate performance can distort the allocation of resources and undermine a company's ability to deliver on its chosen strategy.

5. Corporations must create value for multiple constituencies.

In a free market system, companies succeed only if customers want their products, employees want to work for them, suppliers want them as partners, shareholders want to buy their stock, and communities want their presence. Figuring out how to maintain these relationships and deciding when trade-offs are necessary among the interests of these various groups are central challenges of corporate leadership. Agency theory's implied decision rule—that managers should always maximize value for shareholders—oversimplifies this challenge and leads eventually to systematic underinvestment in other important relationships.

6. Corporations must have ethical standards to guide interactions with all their constituencies, including shareholders and society at large.

Adherence to these standards, which go beyond forbearance from fraud and collusion, is essential for earning the trust companies need to function effectively over time. Agency theory's ambivalence regarding corporate ethics can set companies up for destructive and even criminal behavior—which generates a need for the costly regulations that agency theory proponents are quick to decry.

7. Corporations are embedded in a political and socioeconomic system whose health is vital to their sustainability.

Elsewhere we have written about the damaging and often self-destructive consequences of companies' indifference to negative externalities produced by their activities. We have also found that societal and systemwide problems can be a source of both risk and opportunity for companies. Consider Ecomagination, the business GE built around environmental challenges, or China Mobile's rural communications strategy, which helped narrow the digital divide between China's urban and rural populations and fueled the company's growth for nearly half a decade. Agency theory's insistence that corporations (because they are legal fictions) cannot have social responsibilities and that societal problems are beyond the purview of business (and should be left to governments) results in a narrowness of vision that prevents corporate leaders from seeing, let alone acting on, many risks and opportunities.

8. The interests of the corporation are distinct from the interests of any particular shareholder or constituency group.

As early as 1610, the directors of the Dutch East India Company recognized that shareholders with a 10-year time horizon would be unenthusiastic about the company's investing resources in longer-term projects that were likely to pay off only in the second of two 10-year periods allowed by the original charter. The solution, suggested one official, was to focus not on the initial 10-year investors but on the strategic goals of the enterprise, which in this case meant investing in those longer-term projects to maintain the company's position in Asia. The notion that all shareholders have the same interests and that those interests are the same as the corporation's masks such fundamental differences. It also provides intellectual cover for powerful shareholders who seek to divert the corporation to their own purposes while claiming to act on behalf of all shareholders.

These propositions underscore the need for an approach to governance that takes the corporation seriously as an institution in society and centers on the sustained performance of the enterprise. They also point to a stronger role for boards and a system of accountability for boards and executives that includes but is broader than accountability to shareholders. In the model implied by these propositions, boards and business leaders would take a fundamentally different approach to such basic tasks as strategy development, resource allocation, performance evaluation, and shareholder engagement. For instance, managers would be expected to take a longer view in formulating strategy and allocating resources.

The new model has yet to be fully developed, but its conceptual foundations can be outlined. As shown in the exhibit "Contrasting approaches to corporate governance," the company-centered model we envision tracks basic corporate law in holding that a corporation is an independent entity, that management's authority comes from the corporation's governing body and ultimately from the law, and that managers are fiduciaries (rather than agents) and are thus obliged to act in the best interests of the corporation and its shareholders (which is not the same as carrying out the wishes of even a majority of shareholders). This model recognizes the diversity of shareholders' goals and the varied roles played by corporations in society. We believe that it aligns better than the agency-based model does with the realities of managing a corporation for success over time and is thus more consistent with corporations' original purpose and unique potential as vehicles for projects involving large-scale, long-term investment.

The practical implications of company-centered governance are far-reaching. In boardrooms adopting this approach, we would expect to see some or all of these features:

- greater likelihood of a staggered board to facilitate continuity and the transfer of institutional knowledge

- more board-level attention to succession planning and leadership development

- more board time devoted to strategies for the company's continuing growth and renewal

Contrasting approaches to corporate governance

Theory	Shareholder centered	Company centered
	Agency theory	*Entity theory*
Conception of the corporation	Legal fiction; nexus of contracts; pool of capital	Legal entity; social and economic organism; purposeful organization
Origins of the corporation	Private agreement among property owners to pool and increase capital	Created by lawmakers to encourage investment in long-term, large-scale projects needed by society
Functions of the corporation	Maximize wealth for shareholders	Provide goods and services; provide employment; create opportunities for investment; drive innovation
Purpose of specific corporations	Maximize shareholder value	Business purpose set by the particular company's board
Responsibilities to society	None (fictional entities can't have responsibilities)	Fulfill business purpose and act as a good corporate citizen
Ethical standards	Unclear: whatever shareholders want, or obey law and avoid fraud or collusion	Obey law and follow generally accepted ethical standards
Role of shareholders	Principals/owners of the corporation with authority over its business	Owners of shares; suppliers of capital with defined rights and responsibilities

Nature of shareholders	Undifferentiated, self-interested wealth maximizers	Diverse, with differing objectives, incentives, time horizons, and preferences
Role of directors	Shareholders' agents, delegates, or representatives	Fiduciaries for the corporation and its shareholders
Role of management	Shareholders' agents	Leaders of the organization; fiduciaries for the corporation and its shareholders
Management's objective	Maximize returns to shareholders	Sustain performance of the enterprise
Management's time frame	Present/near term (theory assumes the current share price captures all available knowledge about the company's future)	Established by the board; potentially indefinite, requiring attention to near, medium, and long term
Management performance metrics	Single: returns to shareholders	Multiple: returns to shareholders; company value; achievement of strategic goals; quality of goods and services; employee well-being
Strength	Simple structure permits clear economic argument	Consistent with law, history, and the realities facing managers
Weakness	Principles do not accord with law or good management; shareholders have power without accountability	Principles describe complex relationships and responsibilities; success is difficult to assess

- closer links between executive compensation and achieving the company's strategic goals

- more attention to risk analysis and political and environmental uncertainty

- a strategic (rather than narrowly financial) approach to resource allocation

- a stronger focus on investments in new capabilities and innovation

- more-conservative use of leverage as a cushion against market volatility

- concern with corporate citizenship and ethical issues that goes beyond legal compliance

A company-centered model of governance would not relieve corporations of the need to provide a return over time that reflected the cost of capital. But they would be open to a wider range of strategic positions and time horizons and would more easily attract investors who shared their goals. Speculators will always seek to exploit changes in share price—but it's not inevitable that they will color all corporate governance. It's just that agency theory, in combination with other doctrines of modern economics, has erased the distinctions among investors and converted all of us into speculators.

If our model were accepted, speculators would have less opportunity to profit by transforming long-term players into sources of higher earnings and share prices in the short term. The legitimizing argument for attacks by unaccountable parties with opaque holdings would lose its force. We can even imagine a new breed of investors and asset managers who would focus explicitly on long-term investing. They might develop new valuation models that take a broader view of companies' prospects or make a specialty of valuing the hard-to-value innovations and intangibles—and also the costly externalities—that are often ignored in today's models. They might want to hold shares in companies that promise a solid and continuing return and that behave as decent corporate citizens. Proxy advisers might emerge to serve such investors.

We would also expect to find more support for measures to enhance shareholders' accountability. For instance, activist shareholders seeking significant influence or control might be treated as fiduciaries for the corporation or restricted in their ability to sell or hedge the value of their shares. Regulators might be inclined to call for greater transparency regarding the beneficial ownership of shares. In particular, activist funds might be required to disclose the identities of their investors and to provide additional information about the nature of their own governance. Regulators might close the 10-day window currently afforded between the time a hedge fund acquires a disclosable stake and the time the holding must actually be disclosed. To date, efforts to close the window have met resistance from agency theory proponents who argue that it is needed to give hedge funds sufficient incentive to engage in costly efforts to dislodge poorly performing managers.

The time has come to challenge the agency-based model of corporate governance. Its mantra of maximizing shareholder value is distracting companies and their leaders from the innovation, strategic renewal, and investment in the future that require their attention. History has shown that with enlightened management and sensible regulation, companies can play a useful role in helping society adapt to constant change. But that can happen only if directors and managers have sufficient discretion to take a longer, broader view of the company and its business. As long as they face the prospect of a surprise attack by unaccountable "owners," today's business leaders have little choice but to focus on the here and now.

Further Reading

BELOW ARE SOME OF THE BOOKS and articles that examine themes touched on in this article.

- *Capitalism at Risk: Rethinking the Role of Business,* Joseph L. Bower, Herman B. Leonard, and Lynn S. Paine, Harvard Business Review Press, 2011

- *Firm Commitment: Why the Corporation Is Failing Us and How to Restore Trust in It,* Colin Mayer, Oxford University Press, 2013

- *Fixing the Game: Bubbles, Crashes, and What Capitalism Can Learn from the NFL,* Roger L. Martin, Harvard Business Review Press, 2011

- *The Shareholder Value Myth: How Putting Shareholders First Harms Investors, Corporations, and the Public,* Lynn Stout, Berrett-Koehler, 2012

- **"Focusing Capital on the Long Term,"** Dominic Barton and Mark Wiseman, HBR, January–February 2014

- **"A Global Leader's Guide to Managing Business Conduct,"** Lynn S. Paine, Rohit Deshpandé, and Joshua D. Margolis, HBR, September 2011

- **"The Incentive Bubble,"** Mihir Desai, HBR, March 2012

- **"Managing Investors: An Interview with Sam Palmisano,"** Justin Fox, HBR, June 2014

- **"What Good Are Shareholders?"** Justin Fox and Jay W. Lorsch, HBR, July–August 2012

Originally published in May–June 2017. Reprint R1703B

The CEO View: Defending a Good Company from Bad Investors

A conversation with former Allergan CEO David Pyott
by Sarah Cliffe

David Pyott had been the CEO of Allergan for nearly 17 years in April 2014, when Valeant Pharmaceuticals and Pershing Square Capital Management initiated the hostile takeover bid described in the accompanying article "The Error at the Heart of Corporate Leadership." He was the company's sole representative during the takeover discussions. When it became clear that the bid could not be fended off indefinitely, Pyott, with his board's blessing, negotiated a deal whereby Allergan would be acquired by Actavis (a company whose business model, like Allergan's, was growth oriented).

HBR: Would you describe Allergan's trajectory in the years leading up to the takeover bid?

PYOTT: We'd experienced huge growth since 1998, when I joined as just the third CEO of Allergan and the first outsider in that role. We restructured when I came in and again 10 years later, during the recession. Those cuts gave us some firepower for investing back into the economic recovery. After the recession we were telling the market to expect double-digit growth in sales revenue and around the mid-teens in earnings per share.

Your investor relations must have been excellent.

They were. I am extremely proud to say that we literally never missed our numbers, not once in 17 years. We also won lots of awards from investor-relations magazines. You don't run a business with that in mind, but it's nice to be recognized.

In their article, Joseph Bower and Lynn Paine describe how difficult it is for any company to manage the pressure from investors who want higher short-term returns. You seem to have managed that well—until Valeant showed up. How?

Both buy-side and sell-side investors are like any other customer group. You should listen to what they say and respond when you can. But remember: Asking is free. If they say, "Hey, we want more," you have to be willing to come back with "This is what we can commit to. If there are better places to invest your funds, then do what you need to." Fortunately or unfortunately, I'm very stubborn.

Permit me a naive question: Since Allergan was going strong, why did it make sense to Valeant/Pershing Square to take you over and strip you down? I get that they'd make a lot of money, but wouldn't fostering continued growth make more in the long run?

Different business models. Valeant was a roll-up company; it wasn't interested in organic growth. Michael Pearson [Valeant's CEO] liked our assets—and he needed to keep feeding the beast. If he didn't keep on buying the next target, then the fact that he was stripping all the assets out of companies he'd already bought would have become painfully obvious.

He couldn't do it alone, given his already weak balance sheet, so he brought Ackman in—and Pershing Square acquired 9.7% of our stock without our knowledge. This was meant to act as a catalyst to create a "wolf pack." Once the hedge funds and arbitrageurs get too big a position, you lose control of your company.

I still thought we had a strong story to tell—and I hoped I could get long-term-oriented shareholders to buy new stock and water down the hedge funds' holdings. But almost nobody was willing to up their position. They all had different reasons—some perfectly good ones. It was a lesson to me.

That must have been disappointing.

Yes. It's poignant—some of those same people say to me now, "We miss the old Allergan. We're looking for high-growth, high-innovation stocks and not finding them." I just say, "I heartily agree with you."

Another thing that surprised and disappointed me was that I couldn't get people who supported what we were doing— who understood why we were not accepting the bid, which grossly undervalued the company—to talk to the press. Several people said they would, but then folks at the top of their companies said no. And the reporters who cover M&A don't know the companies well. The people who cover pharma are deeply knowledgeable—but once a company is in play, those guys are off the story day-to-day. So the coverage was more one-sided than we'd have hoped for.

Is the trend toward activist investors something that the market will eventually sort out?

Activist and hostile campaigns have been propelled by extraordinarily low interest rates and banks' willingness to accept very high leverage ratios. Recently investor focus has returned to good old-fashioned operational execution by management. But I do think that investment styles go in and out of fashion. I never would have guessed that when I went to business school.

Do you agree with Bower and Paine that boards and CEOs need to focus less on shareholder wealth and more on the well-being of the company?

Look at it from a societal point of view: A lot of the unrest we've seen over the past year is rooted in the idea that wealthy, powerful people are disproportionately benefiting from the changes happening in society. A lot of companies think that they need to make themselves look more friendly, not just to stockholders but to employees and to society. Having a broader purpose—something beyond simply making money—is how you do that and how you create strong corporate cultures.

I don't believe that strong performance and purpose are at odds, not at all. My own experience tells me that in order for a company to be a really high performer, it needs to have a purpose. Money matters to employees up to a point, but they want to believe they're working on something that improves people's lives. I've also found that employees respond really favorably when management commits to responsible social behavior. I used to joke with employees about saving water and energy and about recycling: "Look, I'm Scottish, OK? I don't like waste, and it saves the company money." That's a positive for employees.

Did that sense of purpose pay off when you were going through the takeover bid?

Absolutely. I left day-to-day operations to our president, Doug Ingram, that year. And we grew the top line 17%—more than $1 billion—the best operating year in our 62-year history. I remember an R&D team leader who came up to me in the parking lot and said, "Are you OK? Is there anything I can do?" I answered him, "Just do your job better than ever, and don't be distracted by the rubbish you read in the media." Employees all over the world outdid themselves, because they believed in the company.

What changes in government rules and regulations would improve outcomes for the full range of stakeholders?

My favorite fix is changing the tax rates. Thirty-five percent is woefully high relative to the rest of the world. If we got it down to 20%, we'd be amazed at how much investment and job creation happened in this country. The high rates mean that we're vulnerable to takeovers that have tax inversion as a motivator. We were paying 26%, and Valeant [headquartered in Canada] paid 3%. I think the capital gains taxes could be changed—in a revenue-neutral way—to incentivize holding on to stocks longer.

Shifting gears again: If a company wants to reorient itself toward long-term growth, what has to happen?

I think it's hard for a CEO to change his or her spots. Some can, but most can't. So in most cases you're going to need a new leader. And the board of directors really has to buy into it, because not only are you changing your strategy, you're changing your numbers. You must have a story to tell, for example: "For the next three years, we're not going to deliver 10% EPS growth. It's going to be 5% while we invest in the future. And that's not going to pay off until after three years, so you'll have to be patient." You have to be very, very clear about it.

And then everyone—the board, the investors, the lab technicians, the salespeople—will watch you to see if you're serious. It will take a lot of fortitude and determination. It's not impossible, but it's extremely difficult.

Originally published in May–June 2017. Reprint R1703B

The Board View: Directors Must Balance All Interests

An interview with Barbara Hackman Franklin by Sarah Cliffe

The 29th U.S. secretary of commerce and chair emerita of the National Association of Corporate Directors, Barbara Hackman Franklin has served on the boards of 14 public and four private companies. She has been cited by the American Management Association as one of the 50 most influential corporate directors in America. She is the president and CEO of Barbara Franklin Enterprises, a consulting firm that advises American companies doing business in international markets.

HBR: Do you agree that an excessive focus on shareholders has become a problem?

FRANKLIN: The short answer is yes. But let me first tell you how I think about corporate governance. I have always viewed it as a tripartite system of checks and balances. Shareholders own shares and elect the board of directors. The board of directors sets policies and hires and fires the CEO. The CEO and management run the company. The power balance among those three parties ebbs and flows over time, but there's always some balance. When I first joined boards of large public companies, three decades ago, CEOs were dominant. Then boards began to assert themselves, and the balance shifted toward them, particularly after Sarbanes-Oxley was passed, in 2002. The balance has shifted again in the past five or six years, toward shareholders.

But there's an added complication, which is activist shareholders, and their increased presence seems to me different from the normal ebb and flow among the three parties. Different and more worrying. This has been a new thing over the past few years. So I agree that the power should now shift back from shareholders and more toward boards and management.

What impact do you see?

The hedge fund activists have affected how other investors behave. I see an increase in pressure from the investment community generally for quarterly earnings, for pushing up the stock price. There's some impact perhaps on strategy development and how resources are being allocated. The idea that we should "think like an activist" pops up from time to time in boardroom conversations.

When Joseph Bower and Lynn Paine sent their article around for comments, one person said that corporate centricity wouldn't be possible unless boards made some substantive changes in how they do their job. Does that sound right to you? If so, what changes?

One thing I like about that article: It defines some of the things that boards should have been doing all along. And some boards are doing them, but maybe not enough. (It's hard to do them if you're experiencing unrelenting pressure for short-term performance.) For example, boards need to have strategy discussions with management and the CEO all year long. It can't be a "once and done" event—strategy needs to be discussed at literally every meeting.

If strategy is on the docket every time, then you can discuss all aspects of it—short-term versus long-term decisions, of course, and whether any decisions need to be revisited. Resource allocation is a part of that. Risk management is a part of that. And underlying the ability to tackle those questions is how the culture in the boardroom works. Is there respect for all voices? Is the CEO willing to listen, interact, and respond? Is there just one agenda: the future well-being of the corporation and its stakeholders, always with an eye to how that will create value for shareholders?

A focus on the short term has led some boards to neglect core responsibilities, such as succession planning. That, too, needs to happen continuously. Board members need to be sure there's a viable bench of CEO candidates, and that means knowing them really well. That way, when you need to make a decision about the next leader, you can match the right candidate to the strategic direction.

Another piece that gets neglected—but is hugely important to this discussion—is good communication. The board and the company need to give shareholders and other stakeholders accurate, timely information. Some shareholders get unnerved when they don't know enough about what's really going on or about the thought process that led to a collective decision. A lot of times when things come unglued, it's the result of poor communication.

Compensation is another big part of the board's job. How should the thinking on that change, if at all?

People talk a lot about "pay for performance." But what does that mean? I think boards need to develop a balanced scorecard for assessing performance, which will then help to determine compensation. If you have a performance scorecard that covers an array of issues, both long term and short term, it's another hedge against short-termism.

Regardless of whether there's a shift away from shareholder centricity, I think boards are going to have to step up because of changes in the business environment that are happening now, as often occurs when we have a new administration and a new Congress.

Bower and Paine believe that extreme shareholder centricity turns boards and executives into order takers rather than fiduciaries and that boards and CEOs must keep the health of the organization— rather than wealth maximization—front and center.

Yes, I agree with that. I have always believed that my fiduciary responsibility was to the corporation, and that includes its stakeholders. The article calls them constituencies, but we're talking about the same thing. You have to include stakeholders as well as shareholders.

There are interesting variations among state-level statutes. In the first place, most state corporation statutes do not require directors to put shareholders first. Rather, it is the body of case law accumulated over several decades that has caused the focus on maximizing shareholder value. And it's worth noting that there are now 28 states whose statutes allow directors to consider the interests of "other constituencies." I believe this is a good thing.

What do you hear CEOs saying about how they balance pressures from various constituencies?

I think there is concern about balancing longer term and short term. Some of us have signed on to these pronouncements claiming that there's too much emphasis on short-termism, whether it's a focus on stock price or on TSR. Too much focus on any single measure is really detrimental to the long-term purposes of a company. Finding the right balance is on all our minds—CEOs as well as board members.

But it's the global business environment that is keeping us up at night.

You've spent a lot of time in boardrooms—is there anything big that you wish Bower and Paine had addressed?

For me, what's missing is a discussion of the appropriate power balance between management and the board. That's easy to define on paper but really difficult in practice. A topic for another day. Maybe once we get the problem of activist investors sorted out, the authors can tackle that.

Originally published in May–June 2017. Reprint R1703B

Finally, Evidence That Managing for the Long Term Pays Off

by Dominic Barton, James Manyika, and Sarah Keohane Williamson

Companies deliver superior results when executives manage for long-term value creation and resist pressure from analysts and investors to focus excessively on meeting Wall Street's quarterly earnings expectations. This has long seemed intuitively true to us. We've seen companies such as Unilever, AT&T, and Amazon succeed by sticking resolutely to a long-term view. And yet we have not had the comprehensive data needed to quantify the payoff from managing for the long term—until now.

New research, led by a team from McKinsey Global Institute in cooperation with FCLT Global, found that companies that operate with a true long-term mindset have consistently outperformed their industry peers since 2001 across almost every financial measure that matters.

The differences were dramatic. Among the firms we identified as focused on the long term, average revenue and earnings growth were 47% and 36% higher, respectively, by 2014, and market capitalization grew faster as well. The returns to society and the overall economy were equally impressive. By our measures, companies that were managed for the long term added nearly 12,000 more jobs on average than their peers from 2001 to 2015. We calculate that U.S. GDP over the past decade might well have grown by an additional $1 trillion if the whole economy had performed at the level our long-term stalwarts delivered—and generated more than five million additional jobs over this period.

Firms focused on the long term exhibit stronger fundamentals and performance

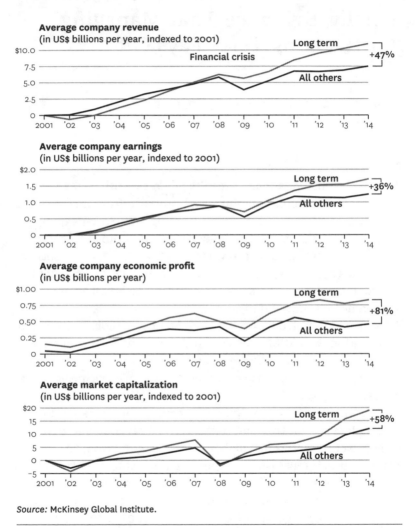

Average company revenue
(in US$ billions per year, indexed to 2001)

Long term

Financial crisis

+47%

All others

Average company earnings
(in US$ billions per year, indexed to 2001)

Long term

+36%

All others

Average company economic profit
(in US$ billions per year)

Long term

+81%

All others

Average market capitalization
(in US$ billions per year, indexed to 2001)

Long term

+58%

All others

Source: McKinsey Global Institute.

Who are these overachievers and how did we identify them? We'll dive into those answers shortly. But first, it's worth pausing to consider why finding conclusive data that establishes the rewards from long-term management has been so hard—and just how tangled the debate over this issue has been as a result.

In recent years we have learned a lot about the causes of short-termism and its intensifying power. We know from FCLT surveys, for example, that 61% of executives and directors say that they would cut discretionary spending to avoid risking an earnings miss, and a further 47% would delay starting a new project in such a situation, even if doing so led to a potential sacrifice in value. We also know that most executives feel the balance between short-term account-ability and long-term success has fallen out of whack; 65% say the short-term pressure they face has increased in the past five years. We can all see what appear to be the results of excessive short-termism in the form of record levels of stock buybacks in the U.S. and historic lows in new capital investment.

But while measuring the increase in short-term pressures and identifying perverse incentives is fairly straightforward, assessing the ultimate impact of corporate short-termism on company per-formance and macroeconomic growth is highly complex. After all, "short-termism" does not correspond to any single quantifiable met-ric. It is a confluence of so many complex factors it can be nearly impossible to pin down. As a result, despite persistent calls for more long-term behavior from us and from CEOs who share our views, such as Larry Fink of BlackRock and Mark Wiseman, the former head of the Canada Pension Plan Investment Board, a genuine debate has continued to rage among economists and analysts over whether short-termism really destroys value.

Academic studies have linked the possible effects of short-termism to lower investment rates among publicly traded firms and decreased returns over a multiyear time horizon. Ambitious work has even attempted to quantify economic growth foregone due to cuts in R&D expenditure driven by short-termism, putting it in the range of about 0.1% per year. Other researchers, however, remain skeptical. How, they ask, could corporate profits in the U.S. remain so high for so long if short-termism were such a drag on performance? And isn't the focus on quarterly results a natural outgrowth of the rigorous corporate governance that keeps executives accountable?

What We Actually Measured—and the Limits of Our Knowledge

To help provide a better factual base for this debate, MGI, working with McKinsey colleagues from our Strategy & Corporate Finance practice as well as the team at FCLT Global, began last fall to devise a way to systemically measure short-termism and long-termism at the company level. It started with developing a proprietary Corporate Horizon Index. The data for this index was drawn from 615 non-finance companies that had reported continuous results from 2001 to 2015 and whose market capitalization in that period had exceeded $5 billion in at least one year. (We wanted to focus on companies large enough to feel the potential short-term pressures exerted by shareholders, boards, activists, and others.) Collectively, our sample accounts for about 60%–65% of total U.S. public market capitalization over this period. To further ensure valid results and to avoid bias in our sample, we evaluated all companies in our index only relative to their industry peers with similar opportunity sets and market conditions and tracked them over several years. We also looked at the proportional composition of the long-term and short-term groups to ensure they are approximately equivalent, so that the differential performance of individual industries cannot bias the overall results, and conducted other tests and controls to ensure statistical robustness.

One final caveat: While we firmly believe our index enables us to classify companies as "long-term" in an unbiased manner, our findings are descriptive only. We aren't saying that a long-term orientation causes better performance, nor have we controlled for every factor that could impact the relationship between those two. All we can say is that companies with a long-term orientation tend to perform better than similar but short-term-focused firms. Even so, the correlation we uncovered between behaviors that typify a longer-term approach and superior historical performance deliver a message that's hard to ignore.

To construct our Corporate Horizon Index, we identified five financial indicators, selected because they matched up with five hypotheses we had developed about the ways in which long- and short-term companies might differ. These indicators and hypotheses were:

- *Investment.* The ratio of capex to depreciation. We assume long-term companies will invest more and more-consistently than other companies.

- *Earnings quality.* Accruals as a share of revenue. Our belief is that the earnings of long-term companies will rely less on accounting decisions and more on underlying cash flow than other companies.

- *Margin growth.* Difference between earnings growth and revenue growth. We assume that long-term companies are less likely to grow their margins unsustainably in order to hit near-term targets.

- *Earnings growth.* Difference between earnings-per-share (EPS) growth and true earnings growth. We hypothesize that long-term companies will focus less on things like Wall Street's obsession with earnings-per-share, which can be influenced by actions such as share repurchases, and more on the absolute rise or fall of reported earnings.

- *Quarterly targeting.* Incidence of beating or missing EPS targets by less than two cents. We assume long-term companies are more likely to miss earnings targets by small amounts (when they easily could have taken action to hit them) and less likely to hit earnings targets by small amounts (where doing so would divert resources from other business needs).

After running the numbers on these indicators, two broad groups emerged among those 615 large and midcap U.S. publicly listed companies: a "long-term" group of 164 companies (about 27% of the sample), which were either long-term relative to their industry peers over the entire sample or clearly became more long-term between the first half of the sample period and the second half, and a baseline group of the 451 remaining companies (about 73% of the sample). The performance gap that subsequently opened between these two groups of companies offers the most compelling evidence to date of the relative cost of short-termism—and the real payoff that arises from managing for the long term.

Trillions of Dollars of Value Creation at Stake

To recap, from 2001 to 2014, the long-term companies identified by our Corporate Horizons Index increased their revenue by 47% more than others in their industry groups and their earnings by 36% more, on average. Their revenue growth was less volatile over this period, with a standard deviation of growth of 5.6%, versus 7.6% for all other companies. Our long-term firms also appeared more willing to maintain their strategies during times of economic stress. During the 2008–2009 global financial crisis, they not only saw smaller declines in revenue and earnings but also continued to increase investments in research and development while others cut back. From 2007 to 2014, their R&D spending grew at an annualized rate of 8.5%, greater than the 3.7% rate for other companies.

Another way to measure the value creation of long-term companies is to look through the lens of what is known as "economic profit." Economic profit represents a company's profit after subtracting a charge for the capital that the firm has invested (working capital, fixed assets, goodwill). The capital charge equals the amount of invested capital times the opportunity cost of capital—that is, the return that shareholders expect to earn from investing in companies with similar risk. Consider, for example, Company A, which earns $100 of after-tax operating profit, has an 8% cost of capital and $800 of invested capital. In this case its capital charge is $800 times 8%, or $64. Subtracting the capital charge from profits gives $36 of economic profit. A company is creating value when its economic profit is positive, and destroying value if its economic profit is negative.

With this metric, the gap between long-term companies and the rest is even bigger. From 2001 to 2014 those managing for the long term cumulatively increased their economic profit by 63% more than the other companies. By 2014 their annual economic profit was 81% larger than their peers, a tribute to superior capital allocation that led to fundamental value creation.

No path goes straight up, of course, and the long-term companies in our sample still faced plenty of character-testing times. During the last financial crisis, for example, they saw their share prices take greater hits than their short-term counterparts. Afterward, however, the long-term firms significantly outperformed, adding an average of $7 billion more to their companies' market capitalization from 2009 and 2014 than their short-term peers did.

While we can't directly measure the cost of short-termism, our analysis gives an indication of just how large the value of what's being left on the table might be. As noted earlier, if all public U.S. companies had created jobs at the scale of the long-term-focused organizations in our sample, the country would have generated at least five million more jobs from 2001 and 2015—and an additional $1 trillion in GDP growth (equivalent to an average of 0.8 percentage points of GDP growth per year). Projecting forward, if nothing changes to close the gap between the long-term group and the others, then the U.S. economy could be giving up another $3 trillion in foregone GDP and job growth by 2025. Clearly, addressing persistent short-termism should be an urgent issue not just for investors and boards but also for policy makers.

Where Do We Go from Here?

Our research is just a first step toward understanding the scope and magnitude of corporate short-termism. For instance, our initial dataset was limited to the U.S., but we know the problem is a global one. How do the costs and drivers differ by regions? Our sample set consists only of publicly listed companies. How do the effects we discovered differ among private companies or among public companies with varying types of ownership structures? Are there metrics that can help predict when a company is becoming too short-term— and how do they differ among industries? Most important, what are the interventions that will prove most effective in shifting organizations onto a more productive long-term path?

On this last point, we and many others have identified steps that executives, boards, and institutional investors can take to achieve a better balance between hitting targets in the short term and operating with a persistent long-term vision and strategy. These range from creating investment mandates that reward long-term value creation, to techniques for "de-biasing" corporate capital allocation, to rethinking traditional approaches to investor relations and board composition. We will return to HBR in coming months with more data and insights into how companies can strengthen their long-term muscles.

The key message from this research is not only that the rewards from managing for the long term are enormous; it's also that, despite strong countervailing pressures, real change *is* possible. The proof lies in a small but significant subset of our long-term outperformers—14%, to be precise—that didn't start out in that category. Initially, these companies scored on the short-term end of our index. But over the course of the 15-year period we measured, leaders at the companies in this cohort managed to shift their corporations' behavior sufficiently to move into the long-term category. What were the practical actions these companies took? Exploring that question will be a major focus for our research in the coming year. For now, the simple fact of their success is an inspiration.

Further Reading

- **"Capitalism for the Long Term,"** Dominic Barton, HBR, March 2011

- **"Focusing Capital on the Long Term,"** Dominic Barton and Mark Wiseman, HBR, January–February 2014

- **"Where Boards Fall Short,"** Dominic Barton and Mark Wiseman, HBR, January–February 2015

- **"The Short Long,"** Andrew G. Haldane and Richard Davies, speech, Bank of England, May 2011

- **"Profits Without Prosperity,"** William Lazonick, HBR, September 2014

- **"Does a Long-Term Orientation Create Value?"** Caroline Flammer and Pratima Bansal, *Strategic Management Journal*, February 2017

- **"Businesses Can and Will Adapt to the Age of Populism,"** the *Economist*, January 2017

Originally published in February 2017. Reprint H03GCC

The New Work of the Nonprofit Board

by Barbara E. Taylor, Richard P. Chait, and Thomas P. Holland

Editor's Note: The new work *of the nonprofit board isn't new anymore—in fact it wasn't very new when the authors wrote this article in the mid-1990s. But the old ways can be deeply entrenched, and the best practices that Taylor, Chait, and Holland describe still haven't been universally adopted—the statistics in the sidebar "The Sorry State of Nonprofit Boards," drawn from a study done 20 years after this article appeared in HBR, prove that. Nevertheless, "old boards" can learn to do the new work, and this piece provides a road map for evolving from "a collection of high-powered people engaged in low-level activities" into a dynamic, goal-driven board focused on advancing the organization's mission, strategic priorities, and long-term welfare.*

EFFECTIVE GOVERNANCE BY THE BOARD of a nonprofit organization is a rare and unnatural act. Only the most uncommon of nonprofit boards functions as it should by harnessing the collective efforts of accomplished individuals to advance the institution's mission and long-term welfare. A board's contribution is meant to be strategic, the joint product of talented people brought together to apply their knowledge and experience to the major challenges facing the institution.

What happens instead? Nonprofit boards are often little more than a collection of high-powered people engaged in low-level activities. Why? The reasons are myriad. Sometimes the board is stymied by a chief executive who fears a strong board and hoards information, seeking the board's approval at the last moment. Sometimes board members lack sufficient understanding of the work of the institution and avoid dealing with issues requiring specialized knowledge. Individual board members may not bring themselves fully to the task of governance, because board membership generally carries little personal accountability. And often the powerful individuals who make up the board are unpracticed in working as members of a team. No matter which cause predominates, nonprofit board members are often left feeling discouraged and underused, and the organization gains no benefit from their talents. The stakes remain low, the meetings process-driven, the outcomes ambiguous, and the deliberations insular. Many members doubt whether a board *can* have any real power or influence.

The key to improved performance is discovering and doing what we call the *new work* of the board. Trustees are interested in results. High-powered people lose energy when fed a steady diet of trivia. They may oblige management by discussing climate control for art exhibitions, the condition of old steam lines, or the design of a new logo, but they get charged up when searching for a new CEO, successfully completing a capital campaign, or developing and implementing a strategic plan. *New work* is another term for work that matters.

The new work has four basic characteristics. First, it concerns itself with crucial, do-or-die issues central to the institution's success. Second, it is driven by results that are linked to defined timetables. Third, it has clear measures of success. Finally, it requires the engagement of the organization's internal and external constituencies. The new work generates high levels of interest and demands broad participation and widespread support.

The New Work Requires New Practices

The new work defies the conventions that have regulated board behavior in the past. Whereas the customary work of a nonprofit board is limited to scrutinizing management, the new work requires

Idea in Brief

Too often, the board of a nonprofit organization is little more than a collection of high-powered people engaged in low-level activities. But that can change, the authors say, if trustees are willing to take on the *new work* of the board. When they perform the new work, a board's members can significantly advance the institution's mission and long-term welfare.

Doing the new work requires a board to engage in new practices. First the board must go beyond rubber-stamping management's proposals and find out what issues really matter to the institution. It can do that by making the CEO paint the big picture of the organization's strategic concerns, by understanding key stakeholders, by consulting experts, and by deciding what needs to be measured in order to judge the institution's performance.

Second, a board doing the new work must take action: the board must not only set policy but also work with management to implement it. Third, the board must go beyond strictly functional organization: the new work requires flexibility and encourages ad hoc arrangements. Finally, board meetings—where boards underperform most visibly—should be driven by goals, not by processes.

The authors give many examples of boards that have successfully embraced the new work. The stakes are high: if boards demonstrated that they can change effectively, the professional staff at the institutions they serve just may follow suit.

new rules of engagement and unorthodox ways of fulfilling a board's responsibilities. The pressures on most nonprofits today are too great for the old model to suffice. Nonprofit leaders can take the following steps to improve board practices:

Find out what matters

Traditionally, nonprofit boards and CEOs have agreed that management defines problems and recommends solutions. A board might refine management's proposals but rarely rejects any. Why? Few trustees know the industry or the institution well enough to do more, and those who do dread being labeled as meddlers or micromanagers. Board members sometimes are made to feel that asking a thorny question or advancing an alternative opinion is disloyal to the administration. A vote on an issue is a vote on the CEO. But how can a reactive, uninformed board know what opportunities the organization is missing? And how much damage must the organization sustain before the board realizes something is amiss?

To do the new work, trustees and management together must determine the important issues and the agenda of the organization. Trustees need to understand what the CEO sees as the critical issues. They also need to know what other stakeholders and industry experts think, because no chief executive knows enough to be a board's sole supplier of information and counsel. Knowledgeable trustees can help inform the CEO's judgment. They can also perform a useful function for the CEO by focusing the organization's attention on issues that are unpopular within it or that fall outside the staff's capabilities. In addition, the board can find out what matters by engaging in the following four sets of activities:

Make the CEO paint the big picture. The litmus test of the chief executive's leadership is not the ability to solve problems alone but the capacity to articulate key questions and guide a collaborative effort to formulate answers. As one member of a museum's board observes, "What I want most from the president are the big ideas." The CEO must be willing to share responsibility, and the board must be willing to follow the CEO's lead—and ask questions. "If you don't do that," says one college's trustee, "the board doesn't really have a clue about what is going on. When a problem arises and the CEO needs the trustees, they won't own the problem or be willing to help solve it."

The CEO should review the organization's foremost strategic challenges annually with the board. The board, for its part, must consider whether the CEO accurately targeted and defined the issues. This is a moment, maybe *the* moment, in which the board adds value. Together, the CEO and the board must agree on the institution's priorities and strategic direction. Those considerations, in turn, will shape the work of the board and its evaluation of the CEO.

The board of a college in the South has formalized this process successfully. At a retreat each January, the CEO and the trustees rank the most important challenges facing the institution. Then the board structures its committees to reflect those priorities. Last year, for example, the board concluded that marketing and technological infrastructure were its top concerns. The board formed task forces of trustees and constituents to study those issues, to specify the decisions the board would have to make during the coming year, and to clarify the board's needs for information and education. At the May board meeting, the task forces provided initial reports, and the board decided how to organize in order to pursue the issues. Trustees also developed measurable expectations for the president that were linked to the board's top concerns.

Get to know key stakeholders. Boards and CEOs have to know what matters to the constituents they serve. The interactions of the old work—which were mostly social events and show-and-tell sessions—will not do. The new work requires two-way communication. As a college president remarks, part of the reason for such communication is "to make the board vulnerable to constituents"—to make it accessible and accountable rather than insulated from the ordinary life of the institution. In that spirit, the boards of several colleges now meet routinely with leaders of student, faculty, and alumni bodies to explore matters of common concern.

Consider the example of a residential treatment center for children with emotional disabilities. When a major benefactor died, the center needed to find new sources of income. While interviewing leaders of social service organizations (a major source of referrals), several board members were shocked to discover that the center was seen as elitist and interested only in easy cases. In fact, many professionals referred the easy cases to less expensive care and assumed that the center would reject the difficult ones. Alarmed by these misperceptions, the trustees formed a task force to guide a public relations effort. The board expanded to include trustees with ties to sources of referrals and strengthened its relationships with other constituents through educational events and joint programming. "I want to make sure this board is never again so out of touch with its community," said the board's chair at the end of the process.

Close ties between the board and constituents unnerve CEOs who are determined to be the board's sole source of information and fear that direct communication between trustees and stakeholders will weaken time-honored lines of authority. That reaction puzzles board members; as one college trustee asks, "Why not have students talk to trustees? What's there to hide? These are our clients. I'm old enough and smart enough to know that some people just want to complain. Trustees are as qualified as the president to interpret the views they express. The closer I get to reality, the better I can sympathize with and help the CEO."

Consult experts. Many nonprofits are susceptible to competitive forces and to changes in public policy. Consider, for example, the impact on museums of cuts in funding by the National Endowment for the Arts, or the effect on hospitals of efforts to reform federally funded health care. Unless trustees understand the basic economics, demographics, and politics of the industry, boards will be hard pressed to separate the trivial from the significant and the good news from the bad. The new work requires learning about the industry from many sources.

One of those sources should be experts on the board itself. Although boards regularly recruit trustees with expertise in functional areas like finance, law, and marketing, the new work requires a board to have more than a few trustees with relevant professional expertise: physicians on a hospital's board, academics on a college's board, social workers on a clinic's board. Expert trustees can guide fellow board members through a foreign culture. For example, one Ivy League institution counted a former university president among its board members. At one point, he criticized his colleagues for second-guessing the administration's disciplining of a fraternity, saying, "I'd be furious if my board did this." The board backed off. And at a liberal arts college, a trustee who was a professor at another school helped educate the board about the complexities of measuring teaching quality and reallocating academic positions from departments with declining enrollments to those with growing demand. At the same time, he helped establish the board's credibility with the faculty.

Another source of knowledge is outside experts. They can help boards understand competition, client demographics, trends in government support, and public policy debates. For example, the board of a Protestant theological seminary faced with declining enrollment conferred with experts on professional education, the economics of religious education, and the demographics of its own denomination. The trustees learned that their denomination's population would continue to decline, further eroding financial support for the seminary and job opportunities for new ministers. On its current course, the institution would be bankrupt in a few years. The seminary decided to leverage the strength of its high-quality faculty by becoming a resource to the broader Protestant community, offering theological education to laypeople and continuing education for church workers and ministers, both on campus and in local churches.

Decide what needs to be measured. Corporate boards typically monitor a limited number of performance indicators. Those vital signs convey the company's overall condition and signal potential problems. Nonprofit boards often lack comparable data, largely because the trustees and the staff have never determined what matters most.

Together, the board and management should identify 10 to 12 critical indicators of success. For a college, that may mean scrutinizing its tuition discount (the average remission the institution gives to students as financial aid). For a museum, it may mean measuring its total return on endowment investments. For a hospital, the board may monitor occupancy rates. Distinctive strategies can suggest novel measures. A boarding school focusing on computer literacy monitored the ratio between students' dial-ups to the campus network and their phone calls from their dorm rooms for pizza delivery. A rising percentage of network calls meant that students were becoming more comfortable with new technology. Using comparable creativity, an orchestra with an aging subscriber base monitored ticket sales to single people in their twenties and thirties who had attended chamber music programs with wine and cheese receptions held afterward.

Graphic comparisons against projections, past performance, or industry norms focus a board's attention on crucial issues and remind trustees that the ultimate goal of the board is to influence those indicators in a positive way. As the CEO of a college in the Midwest says, "We have a set of key performance indicators, explicitly linked to the strategic plan, that are reviewed at every meeting. We even put them on a pocket-size card that trustees can carry around."

Act on what matters

In the world of the old work, the lines were clearly drawn: the board remained on the policy-setting side of the net, management on the implementation side, and so the game of governance was played. In the new work, the board and management are on the same side of the net as partners in both roles. The question is not, Is this an issue of policy or implementation? Rather, the question is, Is the issue at hand important or unimportant, central or peripheral?

Today few nonprofits can risk barring the CEO from policy development or divorcing the board from policy implementation. In a capital campaign, establishing priorities and goals is setting policy, identifying prospects and making calls is implementation. In the search for a new CEO, determining selection criteria is making policy, designing the procedure and conducting the interviews is implementation. In brief, most important matters cannot be subdivided neatly into policy or administration.

In many instances, implementation is far more consequential than formulation. For example, in face-to-face meetings, trustees of a Catholic women's college persuaded affluent older alumnae to support a new institutional focus on serving poor minority women from the inner city. The board of another college, troubled by the decline in students able to pay full tuition, selected three trustees to assist the administration with the design of a marketing strategy aimed at attracting more students able to pay.

In another case, a university owned a commercial radio station. The board questioned how the station fit in with the school's mission. After deciding with the president that the university could turn profits from the sale of the station to better educational use, the trustees negotiated the transaction. Afterward, the president exulted, "This was the board at its best." The board members knew more than the staff about the radio business and about selling a major asset, and they put that knowledge to use.

Involving trustees in policy implementation can be critically important during a crisis. In the aftermath of the scandal at the United Way of America (the CEO used more than a million dollars of United Way money for personal expenses), the board and CEO of one local chapter agreed that each of the trustees would interview five business leaders to learn what the chapter might do to improve community support for an upcoming campaign. The advice was consistent: admit that the national organization had blundered badly, stop all payments to the national headquarters until the charges were resolved, promise that all funds would remain in the community, allow donor-designated contributions, and promise that the board would issue a public report on allocations. The CEO and the trustees accepted those recommendations and inaugurated an intense public-relations effort that engaged every board member. In the end, the campaign was almost as successful as the previous year's and was substantially more successful than those of other chapters in the region. That would not have been the case had the board only set policy.

Organize around what matters

The board's new work must be organized to deal with the institution's priorities. That may seem self-evident, but boards often organize their work in functionally oriented committees (physical plant, finance, public relations) that channel trustees toward low-stakes operational decisions. For the new work to happen, substance must dictate structure. Committees, work groups, and task forces must mirror the institution's strategic priorities.

Teaching an Old Board New Work

Old Work

1. Management defines problems, assesses options, and proposes solutions. Board listens, learns, approves, and monitors.

2. Board sets policy, which management implements. Respective territories are sharply defined; there is little or no border traffic. Domains are decided by organization chart.

3. Structure of standing committees parallels administrative functions. Premium is on permanent structure, established routines. Members occupy functional niches. Board maintains busywork.

4. Board meetings are process driven. Protocol doesn't vary. Function follows form. Emphasis is on transmission of information and reports.

5. Board is a collection of stars. It recruits people with an eye to expertise and status. The CEO cultivates individual relationships and exploits each trustee's talents.

New Work

1. Board and management discover issues that matter, mutually determine the agenda, and solve problems together.

2. Board and management both set policy and implement it. Lines are blurred, borders open. Domains are decided by nature of issue at hand.

3. Structure of board mirrors institution's strategic priorities. Premium is on flexibility, ad hoc arrangements. Members occupy functional intersections. Board creates centers of action.

4. Board meetings are goal driven. Protocol varies with circumstances. Form follows function. Emphasis is on participation and action.

5. Board is a constellation. It recruits team members with an eye to personality and overall chemistry. Board cultivates group norms and collective capabilities of trustees.

For instance, a theological seminary replaced most of its operationally oriented committees with ones that reflected the major goals of the strategic plan: globalizing the curriculum, improving relations with local churches, and providing continuing education for the ministry. The committees included trustees and constituents. One result: on the recommendation of the committee on church relations, the seminary established a clearinghouse to provide local churches with technical assistance in such areas as financial management, adult education, and church governance.

In another example, the board of a preeminent women's college has under active consideration the creation of four "councils" (business affairs, campus affairs, external affairs, and governance and board affairs) as umbrellas for clusters of standing committees. The council on campus affairs, for example, would oversee the activities and orchestrate the annual agendas of the student-life, admissions, and trustee-faculty relations committees, which would meet only as necessary. The council chairs would coordinate the annual agendas of the four councils and suggest strategic issues for in-depth discussion at board meetings.

Task forces that include constituents and nontrustee experts can tackle critical yet discrete matters such as outsourcing certain functions or installing a total quality management program. For example, the board of an independent day school appointed two task forces to explore accreditation issues with the appropriate state and federal agencies. The task forces gathered information about demographic trends, accreditation requirements, and possible legislation that would affect independent schools. At a special Saturday session, the task forces presented their findings, the board discussed whether to seek accreditation and whether to become more selective, *and* the task forces disbanded. The work had been done.

Such "tissue paper" task forces (use and discard) drive the board toward real-time results, multiply leadership opportunities, and prevent longtime members from dominating standing committees. As one college's trustee confesses, "Many of our standing committees don't really shape policy or identify needs. They're an empty ritual, a burden, not an asset. In contrast, task forces are very effective. For example, we're looking at the cost and shape of a marketing plan. A task force helped the board understand the problem and recommended directions. There was a material difference in the sense of ownership."

Focus meetings on what matters

Boards are boards only in meetings, and yet meetings are where boards underperform most visibly. Many trustees think that lack of time is the most significant barrier to a board's ability to perform the new work. In fact, the greater problem is the failure to determine what matters and to let that imperative drive the frequency, format, and duration of board and committee meetings. And if a board can meet only infrequently or for short periods, trustees should consider realistically what they can deliver. The chair, the CEO, and perhaps the executive committee should design each meeting by asking the questions, What is the purpose of this meeting? and How can we organize it to fulfill that purpose? Four common responses will help illustrate the point.

We need more background to make a decision. This answer calls for a discussion led by a moderator. Discussion sessions can engage and educate the entire board about issues facing the institution. The goal is to air views, invite questions, and consider alternatives—not to win an argument. No specific decision is on the table, and no votes are taken.

Consider the case of the college board that was generally concerned—but not sufficiently informed—about the interrelated issues of student quality, tuition charges, and financial aid. Each year, the finance committee, usually under pressure to balance the next year's budget, presented a tuition recommendation to the board. The process afforded no practical opportunity for the board to study the causes and effects of tuition increases. Last year, the board convened explicitly to learn more about the effect of tuition and financial aid decisions on enrollment and student quality, as well as on the bottom line. Subsequently, the board devised principles to govern the finance committee's recommendations for the following year. Those principles included the decision to hold institutionally funded financial aid to below 25% of overall tuition but to use grants to attract better students. The board also decided to increase average class size in order to free up resources to enhance learning partnerships, including student-faculty research projects.

At another university, each of the board's key committees appears once a year before the whole board for a half-day session to present information on a substantive issue or special area. For example, the finance committee led a board session to explain capital budgeting, deferred maintenance, and depreciation of assets. A task force on instructional technology that included faculty and students held a panel discussion to describe the state of the art across the nation and how technology was being used on their campus to transform the learning process. As a result of such sessions, reports the chair, "The whole board becomes more knowledgeable about the issues. The old bean counters on the finance committee now see other aspects of the institution."

We don't know what to do about a current problem. The new work, by definition, grapples with complicated issues that defy easy solutions. Trustees and management must be able to present multiple perspectives and develop solutions that reflect the group's best thinking. A meeting's design is critical to making that happen. Discussion must center on the explicit question at hand, such as, What should be our top three priorities for the capital campaign? or What specific steps can the board take to improve ties to the corporate community?

Small groups create a more comfortable environment for trustees to speak freely. Says one college board member, "I may have a comment worthy of 16 ears, but not one worthy of 60." Small groups provide venues for brainstorming, arenas where there are no dumb questions or insane ideas. A board member of a midwestern university explains, "Before we added small group discussions, all 50 trustees sat passively and listened to a few people impart information. The process was superficial, and substantive participation was limited to the executive committee. Small groups allow everyone to participate genuinely."

We face a crisis. In times of crisis, business-as-usual must be pushed aside to allow the board to concentrate on the matter at hand. Crises might include the loss of a major source of funding, the sudden departure or death of the CEO, the rise of a competitor, or even a split within the board itself.

Focus on the Constellation, Not the Stars

HISTORICALLY, THE PRACTICE of most large, well-established nonprofits has been to recruit stars as board members. The assumption was that a collection of exceptional individuals would equal an exceptional board. The new work of the board cannot be done by a powerful inner circle. Instead, everyone must get involved. That will set off a chain reaction: the more trustees are involved in meaningful work, the more they will know; the more they know, the more they can contribute to the team; and the more they contribute to the team, the more likely the stars will form a constellation.

Too often, an executive committee makes all the important decisions and expects the rest of the board to comply. As one university trustee reports, "The executive committee is a little closed club of trustees who give lip service to inclusiveness but don't really practice it. It's nice, I know, to have all that control, but it's not good for the rest of the board." In those situations, trustees outside the loop of power lose interest.

To function as a team, board members need equal and timely access to information. Agendas, minutes, and background information from task force and committee meetings should be distributed to all trustees, and the board should use technology—conference calls and e-mail—to increase timely communication. Executive committee meetings should be open to all members of the board, and board and committee chairs should be coached to invite reticent trustees to speak, as well as to avoid premature closure of debates.

Given the collaborative character of the new work, prospective trustees should understand that governance is a collective enterprise. They should realize that the board will expect more than attendance, participation, and financial support. The holy trinity of wealth, work, and wisdom (sometimes in just that order!) that has guided the selection of trustees in the past must be changed. Says one trustee of a college in the Midwest, "The operating

For example, a local Alzheimer's Association chapter lost a major grant in 1993 and had no immediate prospects for significant new funding. The chair called a special meeting of the board to discuss restructuring the chapter's services. A review of the mission statement reminded trustees of the organization's purpose; an examination of what it would mean to reengineer the organization helped open up discussion of key issues. By the end of the meeting, board members accepted responsibility for specific tasks to help manage the crisis: explaining the chapter's mission to potential sponsors in principle for selection was to add as many friends as you could, in the hope that some of them would turn out to be helpful. That's a poor approach."

A better approach is to engage potential trustees as members of a task force or a committee so that everyone can become better acquainted—a mutual tryout. Rather than extend an invitation to join the board based chiefly on a prospect's track record, arrange a conversation to explore the fit between the individual and the institution and its board. Some entrepreneurs, industrial captains, and self-employed professionals, for instance, are intolerant of the convoluted decision-making processes and dispersed powers characteristic of most nonprofits. Those individuals, however successful, are unlikely to be effective trustees. Board members should love the organization for what it is as well as for what they hope to make it.

The capacity for team play will be enhanced if new trustees are incorporated as swiftly as possible into the new work of the board. New recruits need to know of recent strategic decisions and current challenges. In addition, the board might accommodate the committee preferences of new trustees so that the rookies can play comfortable positions and thus gain self-confidence and respect from their peers.

A mentoring program that matches a seasoned trustee with a new trustee provides another way to foster fellowship and to engage newcomers faster. On one board, the pair are seated together for the first year so that the mentor can quietly explain the history of issues before the board, answer questions, decipher the board's unwritten rules, and debrief the new trustee after meetings. A more careful approach to the selection of trustees, combined with a mentoring program, can help a board form the constellation it needs to work at peak effectiveness.

the community, exploring the restructuring experiences of other chapters, and examining with staff the best ways to smooth the transition to a smaller, more tightly focused organization.

We need to deal with sensitive governance issues. Executive sessions without the CEO present open lines of communication among trustees. "We have an executive session after each board meeting," says one college trustee. "We feel free to bring up anything at all. This is a time for us to really ask questions and probe." Among the

The Sorry State of Nonprofit Boards

NONPROFIT DIRECTORS OFTEN FALL SHORT in terms of knowledge and experience, and their boards as a whole need more-rigorous planning and procedures. Those are among the conclusions of Stanford researchers who recently surveyed 924 nonprofit directors. Some specific findings:

Directors lack critical skills	**27%** Directors who say that fellow board members lack a strong understanding of the organization's mission and strategy	**32%** Directors who are not satisfied with the board's ability to evaluate the organization's performance
Boards lack formal processes	**42%** Boards without an audit committee	**69%** Boards without a succession plan for the CEO or the executive director
Fundraising is overemphasized	**90%** In organizations that require directors to fundraise, board members who say that task is at least as important as their other duties	**42%** In organizations that require directors to donate, boards with a "give or get" (donate or raise) minimum
Upheaval is common	**69%** Organizations that have experienced at least one serious governance problem in the past decade	**23%** Boards that have asked the executive director to leave or have faced his or her unexpected resignation

Source: "2015 Survey on Board of Directors of Nonprofit Organizations," by David F. Larcker, William F. Meehan III, Nicholas Donatiello, and Brian Tayan.

questions a board might entertain in an executive session are, Did we deal with important issues? How did the meeting go? Can we better serve the CEO? Differences of opinion among trustees or between the board and the CEO can be treated more candidly in an executive session. Says one board member of a women's college in the South, "If there are sensitive issues, the executive session gives us a chance to counsel one another."

These examples of the new work and new structures are far from exhaustive. Boards should experiment with different formats for different purposes. Use what works.

Leading the Way

Trustees protest regularly that artists, academics, physicians, and other professionals stubbornly resist change. Yet governing boards are among the least innovative, least flexible elements of many nonprofits. Boards are as reluctant to forsake committees as faculty members and physicians are to eliminate departments. Trustees resist varied formats for board meetings more than musicians resist novel formats for concerts. And board members oppose new membership criteria as strongly as teachers oppose nontraditional certification.

This hypocrisy was plain to the chair of a midwestern university's board. "It's tough for a group like this to be self-conscious. They're classic CEOs. They can tell stories about empowerment and team building, but that's not how they got where they are. They are uncomfortable with questions like How are we doing? and How should we improve? Most of our members are heavy into productivity. The board isn't hesitant to ask faculty and administrators to answer these questions. The board wants everyone else's time to be more efficient and effective, but the board should look for ways to improve, too."

Too often, trustees assume that organizational success proves that the board has performed well, even when there is little evidence that the board played a significant role, and even when staff members say privately that the success was achieved *despite* the board. "Most boards have the attitude," a trustee of a women's college notes, "that if it ain't broke, don't fix it, but I think it's better to fix it before it breaks." A sympathetic explanation for the reluctance of most boards to experiment with substantial governance reforms would be the trustees' desire to do no harm. A less charitable explanation would be the trustees' desire to do no work.

Moving to the new work takes work. As the CEO of a midwestern university recounted after the institution's board had changed, "It required getting people out of their little corners, the areas that they had learned and owned. They wanted to work on what they knew best and leave the rest to others. They had to rotate around and learn everything in order to govern the organization. They've moved from being just guardians of the physical plant, overseers of the administration, and suits with deep pockets."

Boards across the nonprofit sector are calling on institutions to change. As trustees demand evidence of productivity gains, efficient processes, and enhanced outcomes, they should model the behavior they seek in others. If boards demonstrate the capacity to discard shibboleths, dismantle old structures, and desert deeply ingrained modes of operation, the professional staff may follow suit. If the board does not do the new work, the trustees' hypocrisy will be blatant, and the value added by the board will be too meager to inspire organizational reform.

Originally published in September–October 1996. Reprint 96509

Dysfunction in the Boardroom

by Boris Groysberg and Deborah Bell

FOR YEARS women have sought greater representation on corporate boards. And most boards say they want more diversity. So why did women hold only 16.6% of *Fortune* 500 board seats in 2012? And why, for the past six years, has that percentage been relatively flat, increasing by just two points, according to data from the research firm Catalyst?

Patience has started to wear thin, especially in Europe. Having seen little progress with voluntary efforts, several countries, including Belgium, France, Iceland, Italy, Norway, Spain, and the Netherlands, have enacted legislation that calls for a minimum percentage of female directors on boards. The European Union is considering mandating quotas as well.

It's unclear why women have not made greater inroads. Board appointments and dynamics remain largely a black box; not much research has been done on the selection and appointment process or on the differences between women's and men's experiences as directors. To learn more, in 2010 we began a series of annual surveys in partnership with WomenCorporateDirectors and Heidrick & Struggles. In this article we reveal the findings of an analysis of qualitative data from the first survey.

We were especially interested in the backgrounds, trajectories, and interactions of female directors—who are the women who get onto boards, and what do they encounter there? So our sample was drawn mainly from female corporate directors; we included a smaller number of male directors as a benchmark. (Overall the survey had a response rate of 42%, with 294 women and 104 men from private and public companies participating.) Also, because the vast majority of the sample consisted of U.S. directors (80% of the women and 83% of the men), the findings largely present a picture of American boards. While our survey has these and other limitations, it still offers several interesting perspectives.

In the following pages, we'll share a profile of the female board member that emerged; what the directors surveyed had to say about the benefits of diversity and about the dynamics between men and women on boards; and some best practices for recruiting and managing diverse boards. In the process, we'll discuss three key themes we discovered in the data:

- Women had to be more qualified than men to be considered for directorships. Women also seemed to pay a higher personal price to become board members than men did.

- Although boards say they like diversity, they don't know how to take advantage of it. We found a stark disconnect between female directors' experiences and their male colleagues' perceptions. Women told us they were not treated as full members of the group, though the male directors were largely oblivious to their female colleagues' experience in this regard.

- Great talent alone is not enough to create a well-functioning board. Boards need formal processes and cultures that leverage each individual member's contribution as well as the directors' collective intellect.

Portrait of the Female Director

In our study, we observed some distinct patterns. The female directors tended to be younger than the male directors—probably because, on average, the women had joined boards relatively recently, whereas

Idea in Brief

Though boards claim they strive for diversity, the number of female directors remains low; women held only 16.6% of *Fortune* 500 board seats in 2012. To find out why—and learn about the women appointed to boards and their experiences—Harvard Business School's Groysberg and organizational researcher Bell teamed up with Heidrick & Struggles and WomenCorporateDirectors to conduct annual surveys of board members. In this article they reveal the findings of their 2010 survey of 294 women and 104 men, presenting a profile of the typical female director, what directors thought about the benefits of diversity and the dynamics between men and women on boards, and best practices for recruiting and managing directors.

Three themes emerged from the data: (1) Women had to be more qualified than men to be considered for boards. Contrary to popular belief, female directors had more operational and leadership experience than male directors. (2) Boards don't know how to leverage diversity. The women said they were not treated as full members of the group, though the men were largely oblivious to this problem. (3) Great talent is not enough to create a great board. Boards need processes and cultures that encourage inclusiveness as well as diversity.

the men had served on boards longer. Seventy-six percent of the female directors (versus 69% of the male directors) were employed in an operational role; 68% (versus 51% of the male directors) were in a lead role, like CEO, president, or partner. These findings suggest that to receive invitations to boards, women might need to be more accomplished than men. They also contradict the popular belief that female board members have mostly nonoperational or support-function experience.

Another distinction we discovered between the backgrounds of female and male directors was that by and large, the women on boards worked for private corporations, not public ones. A majority of the male board members worked for private corporations as well, but a higher percentage of the men worked for public companies—likely a reflection of the fact that fewer women occupy the C-suites of public companies.

The data also indicate that female board members may have made different trade-offs on their way to the top. In comparison with male directors, fewer female directors were married and had children. A larger percentage of the women were divorced—suggesting they may have incurred greater personal costs. We found similar patterns in our 2012 survey.

We were curious to learn about the aspirations of corporate directors, who by most standards have reached the pinnacle of career success. We found that a somewhat higher proportion of women than men (92% and 86%, respectively) described themselves as ambitious. In addition, contrary to gender stereotypes, 91% of the women versus 70% of the men reported that they enjoyed having power and influence.

On average, the women in our survey were serving on two boards and the men on three. Given that, it wasn't surprising that over half the female directors wanted to serve on more boards. (A smaller percentage of the men did.) But the women also expressed greater overall career aspirations. Twenty-seven percent of the female directors wanted to lead or continue leading a company, compared with 19% of the men. Although female directors' younger age may account for some of the difference, it doesn't fully explain it: Twenty-nine percent of the women who actively aspired to the top job were age 60 to 70, whereas only 10% of the men with similar aspirations were. Such ambition at a time of life when most professionals are winding down their careers suggests that women, whose opportunities have consistently been more restricted, may wish to extend the length of their careers with an eye to finally attaining the most-coveted roles.

We also wanted to know what strengths directors would say they brought to their boards and, by implication, what skill sets and areas of expertise they thought were most important to board operations and dynamics. Asked to write in their strengths, the men and women gave remarkably similar answers. One significant difference was that a lot more women than men cited the ability to communicate effectively. Many female directors noted that they were more likely than their male counterparts to ask tough questions or move boardroom discussions forward in skilled and

How female and male directors perceive their strengths

We asked survey respondents to write in what their strengths as board members were. Here are the traits and skills they noted.

	% of women	% of men
Industry and business experience	38	43
Leadership and strategic vision	30	27
Board and governance experience	25	24
Communication	25	17
Finance and investment expertise	24	29
Relationship skills and people management	18	16
Operations experience	14	22
Marketing and sales	13	9
Preparation and organization	10	1
Risk management	5	1
Global experience	5	16
M&A	3	5
Technology expertise	3	3
HR and talent management	3	5
Commitment and passion	3	6

effective ways. (See the chart "How female and male directors perceive their strengths.")

Another notable difference was the greater percentage of men who cited global experience as a strength. In our work with directors and high-level executives, we've found that women are often not considered for international assignments, because of the assumption that women with families find it more difficult than men with families to relocate or travel for extended periods. The unfortunate consequence is that women don't get equal access to international roles.

Golf, Anyone?

MEN HAVE LONG BUILT AND PERPETUATED networks through informal social gatherings and activities—like golf—at which they can cultivate beneficial relationships and make business deals.

We found that the percentage of male directors who golfed (40%) was twice that of female directors who did (20%). Among the CEOs in the study, the difference was slightly greater: 40% of the men and 17% of the women played the game. We also saw that among the women, the percentage of non-CEOs who golfed was higher than the percentage of CEOs who did.

Those data, in combination with our findings on board members' perspectives, suggest that some women who play golf may feel compelled to do so to help advance their careers. Up-and-coming female professionals may take up the sport to increase their visibility and thus the chances they'll be considered for promotions and board positions. And women who already occupy the CEO's office may play to avoid being left out of important discussions that happen outside the executive suite and the boardroom.

Although there are women who enjoy golf, we have also heard many stories that support this hypothesis. One female board member said that when she achieved her first C-suite role, several of her male colleagues advised her: "If you don't want to be excluded from some of the things we do, you're going to need to learn how to golf and start golfing with us." Other women reported that their male colleagues made a lot of important decisions together on the golf course—preempting the opportunity to discuss them at formal meetings. Another female director underscored the point: "Golf was amazingly helpful to my career. I would be the only woman on a men's golf trip. It built great camaraderie and relationships—and respect. It put me on the same playing field as everybody else."

Women shouldn't *have* to take up a sport just to be treated as equals, however. This is not a productive dynamic. Golf reinforces the tradition of the old boys' club. Boards will not become more inclusive if women are forced to play it in order to be selected, heard, and consulted in decision making. Boards must cultivate inclusive, collegial, and respectful relationships among members. Backroom decision making should not be tolerated.

Curiously, more men than women listed operations experience as a strength, even though a greater percentage of the women held operational roles or were leading a company. We cannot say why with certainty, but their answers indicate that women may place a higher value on personal skills, such as leadership and communication, than on role-related experience.

To learn more about the factors that may inform directors' perspectives, we asked about their outside interests. We found substantial differences between women and men. Though both named sports most frequently, men did so at a much higher rate. (See the sidebar "Golf, Anyone?") What was also striking was the higher percentage of women than men who named arts and culture, travel, and philanthropy and community service as outside interests. (See the chart "Directors' outside interests.")

How might these differences affect the way female and male directors form and maintain connections with other directors? Could the lack of common interests make it harder for female and male board members to identify with and relate to one another? Or could these differences be enriching?

Directors' outside interests

To learn what shaped board members' perspectives, we asked directors about their nonwork interests and activities.

	% of women	% of men
Sports	70	90
Travel	49	30
Arts and culture	42	17
Reading	39	38
Philanthropy and community service	26	16
Family and friends	24	22
Food and wine	12	6
Gardening	10	2
Education	4	11

The Benefits of Diversity

According to research by our HBS colleagues Robin Ely and David Thomas, organizations have three major approaches to diversity. We've found that boards' approaches to diversity are similar. They may pursue it as a way to:

1. Institute fairness and rebuke discrimination. Government interventions, whether mandatory (quotas) or voluntary (targets or disclosure reporting recommended by the SEC), have sensitized most boards to the fairness argument for diversity.

2. Build a deeper understanding of and access to desirable customer bases and markets, such as female consumers.

3. Incorporate new perspectives and generate learning. When this is the goal of a board, diversity is integrated into all its practices and informs all discussions and decisions, producing the greatest impact.

To better understand what directors think gender diversity can offer boards, we asked respondents whether women bring special attributes to the role. Ninety percent of the female directors thought they did, compared with 56% of the male directors. Below are the attributes respondents cited, along with representative comments.

While slightly more than half of the male directors said that women bring a fresh perspective to the boardroom, 19% said that gender should not be a factor when selecting directors; instead, selection should be based solely on qualifications and experience. One male director explained, "Women—and any board member—should be judged on their background and skills, not because they have attributes based on gender, race, etc." Another stated, "People bring special attributes, and they are not related to diversity." And a third offered this view: "Any shareholder wants the most qualified board members they can get. Diversity is a plus."

Many people have no doubt that women account for more than 16.6% of the pool of highly qualified potential directors, so the

34% of women and 57% of men say	*29% of women and 3% of men say*	*20% of women and 3% of men say*	*8% of women and 11% of men say*
Women bring fresh perspectives and diversity of thought.	**Women are more willing than men to ask questions and challenge the status quo.**	**Women are more collaborative and inclusive.**	**Women have greater empathy and interpersonal skills.**

"Our experiences as mothers and daughters provide a different view of issues."
–A FEMALE DIRECTOR

"Women have a different perspective on life and therefore on how to conduct business."
–A MALE DIRECTOR

"Women bring knowledge of female buyers' behavior."
–A FEMALE DIRECTOR

"We're not afraid to call a cat a cat and bring up difficult questions. And we can't leave the room without resolving an issue."
–A FEMALE DIRECTOR

"Many senior businesswomen have overcome challenges on their path to success, more so than men. Maybe because of this, many women bring a stronger sense of objectivity to the boardroom. In my experience, it is more often the women who are courageous in difficult conversations and difficult decisions."
–A FEMALE DIRECTOR

"Women tend to be more inclusive and work to be sure everyone is heard."
–A FEMALE DIRECTOR

"Women bring consensusbuilding skills."
–A MALE DIRECTOR

"Women start negotiations at point 40 or 60 and achieve results; men start at point 0 or 100 and argue to argue."
–A FEMALE DIRECTOR

"Women tend to be more sensitive to cultural dynamics and to people's strengths, weaknesses, motivations, and potential."
–A FEMALE DIRECTOR

"Women have more emotional intelligence."
–A MALE DIRECTOR

"Women think about the people behind the numbers."
–A FEMALE DIRECTOR

question remains: Why aren't more women on boards? One female director offered this explanation: "Women are not thought of first as candidates unless a board is looking for gender diversity specifically." Another shared her experience: "I'm not part of the old boys' network. Directorships go to people who are known. I've been so busy leading my company and raising my family that I'm less well known." And a third lamented, "Boards still prefer pale, stale, and male!"

Gender and Board Dynamics

Though boards say they want diversity, what happens once women get on them? Eighty-seven percent of female directors reported facing gender-related hurdles. The obstacles fell into four major categories, listed here along with examples of the types of comments we heard most.

We also asked the male directors if female directors face hurdles that men do not. The majority—56%—said no. Those who answered yes named the four types of barriers listed on next page (with a sampling of their comments).

According to some women's accounts, many male directors seem unaware that they may create hostile board cultures, fail to listen to female directors or accept them as equals, and require them to continually reestablish their credentials.

One female board member gave the following example: A highly successful and accomplished woman in financial services was asked

---

Four types of obstacles women say they face

21% of women say	*20% of women say*	*20% of women say*	*5% of women say*
Not being heard and listened to	**Not being accepted as an equal or as part of the "in" group**	**Establishing credibility**	**Stereotyped expectations of women's behavior**
"I often feel that I'm not heard and that I need to put more effort into making sure that others hear and understand my point of view."	"It's been a challenge earning respect and being treated as an equal member, particularly with older board members."	"As a woman, you have a longer road to build credibility."	"I'm always seen as 'the voice of women.'"
"I have to yell for them to hear me."	"I'm consistently not included in informal gatherings, such as golf games and dinner, by some male board members."	"I have to establish my credentials over and over; it never stops."	"I'm expected to hold the ethical compass for the board and lead on women's initiatives."
		"It's work to make sure the male members feel there is value in my opinion."	

Four types of obstacles men say women face

33% of men say	28% of men say	22% of men say	14% of men say
Limited access to and acceptance on boards because of weaker networks and the old boys' club	Lack of experience and industry knowledge	Bias and prejudice	Having to work harder to prove themselves
"The good old boys' network remains."	"In tech there aren't many women with the relevant leadership and experience qualifications."	"Women do better on boards when they behave more like men."	"Women must spend a longer time than men do earning the trust of men."
"Women's more-limited networks have hurt their ability to gain access to boards."	"Highly qualified women directors are in great demand and tend to stretch themselves very thin. Minorities are the same."	"There's a perspective that women's experiences aren't as valuable."	"Older male directors tend not to listen as closely to female input."

to join the board of a growing multibillion-dollar public company. She was its first and, for many years, only woman director. She brought greatly needed financial expertise to the board as well as a deep understanding of the company's industry, yet she routinely felt shut out and stifled during meetings. Her questions were greeted not with respectful collegiality but as intrusions into the "real" conversation among the male board members.

In fact, the CEO and chairman and other male directors had taken her aside many times and asked her to be "less vocal" and to "stop arguing her point" during meetings. She related how this behavior surfaced during meetings, too, recalling one in particular at which she was pursuing a line of questions about a strategic decision when a male director interrupted her and exclaimed, "You're behaving just like my daughter! You're arguing too much—just stop!"

This story illustrates the kind of experience that may have led female directors to cite the failure of their board colleagues to listen

The View Outside the U.S.

THOUGH THIS ARTICLE IS BASED ON our 2010 survey results, which focused mostly on boards in the United States, we have since expanded the geographic reach of our survey. In 2012 it covered 59 countries, and 44% of the female directors and 71% of the male directors who responded were from outside the United States.

When we compared the U.S. and non-U.S. female directors from 2012, we found many similarities and a few notable differences. (The profile of the 2012 U.S. female board member looked a lot like the general profile of the 2010 female director described in this article.) In 2012, both U.S. and non-U.S. female directors cited industry knowledge, strategy, and financial experience as their top three strengths. Both groups had previously served on similar numbers and types (public versus private) of boards. The typical non-U.S. woman director, however, was currently sitting on a greater number of boards—twice as many as her U.S. counterpart. The female directors from outside the United States were also younger than the Americans. One possible explanation for these differences is that opportunities and demand for female directors may be greater in countries with quotas.

There were also notable variations in the two groups' personal profiles: A greater percentage of female directors outside the U.S. were married and had children, and those with children had slightly more. And more female directors from the U.S were divorced, even after adjusting for country differences in divorce rates. While there are no simple explanations for these differences, we can't help wondering if the fact that the U.S. lags behind other countries in providing paid maternity and parental leave and access to affordable, high-quality child care plays a role. In fact, the U.S. is among a handful of countries that do not mandate paid maternity or parental leave. What would happen if parents were able to take paid leave at the birth of a child and have greater access to quality and affordable care as their children grew? What would be the outcome not only for family life and health but also for both women's and men's careers?

---

to them more often than any other barrier. The fact that few men recognized this dynamic suggests a stark disconnect between female directors' experiences and their male colleagues' perceptions.

In addition, far more male than female directors (28% versus 4%) pointed to a lack of board experience and industry knowledge as a handicap for women, but our findings indicate that men and women may come at the qualifications question from very different perspectives. Men seemed to view inexperience as a fixed and disqualifying trait, whereas women saw it as surmountable—something that could be addressed through learning and development. The high percentage of female directors who held operational roles and were leading organizations implies another disconnect—this one between women's qualifications and men's perceptions.

Diversity in Practice

In their responses to our survey, both male and female directors repeatedly named open communication, well-run general meetings, a candid but collegial tenor, and productive relationships with senior management as attributes of a successful board. Yet research suggests that too many boards ignore the need for those qualities, and recent efforts to overhaul governance have clearly failed to address the question of how to compose a knowledgeable, inclusive body that possesses them.

We studied a large company that was being split into two public companies for which two new boards had to be created. The chairman, who had long championed diversity, was spearheading the process. He appointed a special team to create an objective, transparent method for selecting the directors. After reviewing the roles and responsibilities of each board and the natures of the new businesses, the team derived lists of the skill sets each board needed. Then it created a model containing the dimensions critical to a high-performing board, from functional and industry expertise to behavioral attributes. This approach led both companies to recruit boards that were diverse not only in gender but also in skills—demonstrating that when a firm builds a board using a rigorous assessment of the qualities it needs to carry out its governance task, rather than personal networks, the board is better equipped to execute its functions.

Though more research is needed to measure the impact of different practices on board performance, we have encountered several

Quotas and the Men Who Like Them

WHILE SEVERAL COUNTRIES HAVE PASSED legislation requiring boards to meet certain thresholds for female membership and others are considering such mandates, quotas remain a contentious and controversial subject. A central question is whether they have an overall positive or negative effect on board and company performance and under what conditions. The fact is, we do not yet truly know the effects of quotas. What we do know is that many myths and misconceptions infuse the debate, and more in-depth research is critically needed.

Our 2012 survey results reveal that—contrary to popular belief—men in countries with quotas supported them in higher numbers than men in countries without them. The women's response was even more emphatic: Nearly all the female directors from countries with quotas agreed they were effective, versus about half of the female directors from countries without quotas.

We are currently conducting additional research to help us better understand these findings and the experiences of boards and directors in countries with quotas. One dynamic that may be at play: Satisfaction levels are higher for both women and men in work groups with greater gender balance. Furthermore, in some cases, lower-performing board members may be managed out to create room for new female directors, increasing the board's effectiveness. Men may initially oppose or be highly wary of quotas, but once they're enacted, some men might experience the benefits and satisfaction levels associated with gender-balanced groups.

Percentage of directors who believe quotas are an effective tool for increasing diversity

	% of women	% of men
In countries with quotas	95	43
In countries without quotas	48	23

(detailed on the next page) that boards have used to become more effective. Practices like these help break down obstacles that hinder directors from being fully integrated into boards and contributing to their potential.

1. Build and strengthen group dynamics.	2. Recruit more female and diverse director candidates.	3. Develop more female and diverse candidates internally.	4. Conduct rigorous and regular board assessments and evaluations.
Provide communication and team-building training for members, especially new directors.	Establish a strategic plan for board succession that includes deep discussions of diversity.	Make talent management part of the board's strategic focus to ensure that the company's most important assets are maximized.	Establish a culture of accountability and responsibility.
Engage all members in regular social activities like board dinners and annual retreats.	Broaden the definition of diversity to include experience, skills, capabilities, perspectives, and behavioral attributes needed by the board, and institute rigorous, objective selection processes based on them.	Recruit, develop, and promote a diverse set of candidates at every level of the organization.	Implement consistent and transparent processes to address conflicts between members.

Deal with undesirable behavior of board members. |
| Add conference calls, video chats, and opportunities for additional reporting between meetings. | | Develop a pipeline of future leaders and board members through director advocacy, mentorship, and training. | Act on board reviews and remove poorly performing directors. |

After all, as our data suggest, it takes more than great talent to make a great board. Talent alone cannot overcome dysfunctional dynamics. Companies increasingly recognize the distinction between diversity and inclusiveness: Diversity is counting the numbers; inclusiveness is making the numbers count. Boards need to improve on both dimensions.

Originally published in June 2013. Reprint R1306F

The Board's New Innovation Imperative

by Linda A. Hill and George Davis

THE CHALLENGE OF LEADING INNOVATION is bringing about a sea change in corporate governance. Boards, once the dependably cautious voices urging management to mitigate risk, are increasingly calling for breakthrough innovation in the scramble for competitive advantage. We see this shift playing out across industries—notably at such companies as Ford, Coca-Cola, Nestlé, and Unilever, which are all struggling to address slowing sales in their core businesses.

Embracing innovation and its inherent risks requires that boards and senior management develop new ways of working together. As Mark Ganz, the CEO of Cambia Health Solutions—a company at the forefront of innovation in the health care space—told us, board meetings no longer consist of PowerPoint presentations by management followed by a few perfunctory questions from the board. "The model has changed," he explained. "We now bring the board ideas that are not fully baked and say, 'Help us with this.'" It took some time for the board to realize that management was asking not for the answer but for engagement, he said, but "once they got used to it, it dramatically improved the board-management partnership and the value board members bring to the work of the company."

The desire to create new and different ways of working is not always accompanied by the ability to do so, however. Adopting new roles and norms feels uncomfortable—even unnatural—to most people. To help address this knowing-doing gap, we spoke with directors and CEOs from a range of industries about their boards' capacity to support innovation and risk management. The results were sobering, though the tide seems to be turning. A few of the directors in our study were clearly laggards, even going so far as to argue that innovation was irrelevant in their very mature industries. A handful were trailblazers, like Mark Ganz. The majority were just beginning to work their way through the challenges of governing innovation, some more deliberately and successfully than others.

Through our research, we identified the common obstacles most boards face and gleaned insight into how boards can reshape their roles to effectively foster and support the kind of innovation that leads to substantial growth.

Why Boards Struggle with Innovation

Boards increasingly believe that to fulfill their obligation to ensure the long-term well-being of their companies, they have to support management in developing a compelling innovation strategy. And that means learning to embrace risk while continuing to mitigate and manage it as much as possible. In this inverted risk paradigm, boards are discovering that avoiding risk is the riskiest proposition of all. Paula Price, a director at Accenture, Dollar General, and Western Digital Corporation, told us that boards should aim to develop the organization's "capacity to pivot" into uncharted territory with new products, services, business models, or ways of organizing or getting work done. Standing still or waiting to see how things turn out are not considered serious options in today's often tumultuous environment. A member of one automobile company's board confessed that they had discouraged management from making the leap to electric cars for years; now he feared that the company was playing catch-up.

CEOs and top management appropriately have more power than board members over corporate affairs and major decisions. But without the full support of the board, management is unlikely to take the

Idea in Brief

The Situation

As firms scramble for competitive advantage, boards—once the cautious voices tempering management's—are now calling for breakthrough innovation.

The Challenge

Directors face four concerns in governing innovation: an outdated risk agenda, insufficient time, lack of expertise, and a relationship with management that needs retuning.

The Solution

To bolster out-of-the-box thinking, boards should promote diversity among members. They should foster "creative abrasion" to keep ideas flowing and rethink traditional methods of governing. And they must learn to embrace and encourage risk.

---

big bets required to innovate. What frustrations do board members report when asked about fulfilling their growing obligation to govern innovation? We found four main concerns:

An outdated innovation and risk agenda

Most board members report that the lion's share of their attention around innovation goes toward improving the organization's capacity to execute its current strategy—that is, innovation to sustain the core: developing product line extensions, reducing cost structures to maintain healthy operating margins, improving customer-intimacy and -centricity to address rising customer expectations, and responding to new regulatory regimes and cybersecurity threats.

At the same time, these board members realize that doing the same things better, faster, and more cheaply is not enough. It is not enough, for instance, to make improvements that reduce costs in the supply chain. Companies are now trying to deploy digital supply chains that will allow them to offer different value propositions to customers and even create new business models. As one director put it, "Significant disruption is taking place, and whatever company is at the top today will not be at the top in 10 years. [We] must differentiate ourselves." Another observed that his board's "bias for short-term results" was stifling innovation; instead of pursuing breakthrough initiatives, the company was focused on evolutionary ones. Many directors acknowledged that it was not easy for CEOs to make the bold moves required to keep their companies competitive—especially given the growing demands of activist investors—and that boards were not doing enough to encourage management to pursue admittedly riskier initiatives that could reinvent the business.

Insufficient time

Making time for innovation as an ongoing topic of boardroom conversation is a luxury few board members feel they have. Especially in industries undergoing regulatory changes, such as financial services, energy, and health care, directors reported feeling "overwhelmed" simply attending to the basics of compliance and financial monitoring. Even companies that were performing well struggled to dedicate time to innovation activities. Hasbro CEO Brian Goldner acknowledged the challenge: "It's easy to focus only on the core business when it's going great, but you have to find board time to focus on growth and disruptive activities." Directors we spoke with understood the need to invest in strategic discussion and debate about innovation—as another CEO put it, "To think you can sit in the boardroom and talk strategy once a year means you're out of the game and out to lunch"—yet competing pressures on their attention made it hard to find the time for proper consideration.

Lack of expertise

Many directors—particularly CEOs—express frustration that their boards lack the level of industry expertise and innovation experience necessary to make well-informed risk-reward assessments about proposals. One CEO we spoke with said he actually avoided innovation discussions with the board because he believed that the directors "were too far from the market" to assess the true expected value of a particular innovation project.

Asking the Thorny Questions

TODAY'S BOARDS NEED TO RIGOROUSLY challenge management if they want to ensure that their companies are thinking boldly enough about innovation. Here are some questions that we recommend boards ask themselves:

- Are we devoting enough time to innovation in our board meetings?

- What is our risk appetite? Is it aligned with that of management? What message do our leadership and culture send to the rest of the organization about risk and innovation?

- Have we agreed on metrics to evaluate innovation efforts?

- What is our response when an innovation initiative fails? Are we encouraging or discouraging management to experiment?

- Does our board have the diversity of talent, perspective, and style to make tough choices on innovation? Are we hearing from everybody?

- What are we doing to ensure that we are aware of the cutting edge in our industry and in adjacent ones? Is it time to create some advisory committees to support the board?

- Are our board meetings about innovation truly a dialogue, or more of a presentation?

- Would senior leaders describe their relationship with us as a partnership? Would management describe us as supportive of its efforts to innovate?

- Are we sending a clear message to management about the need to be bold, not only to protect the core business but also to reimagine the business and move us to a new future?

Unproductive interactions between the board and management
Historically, companies have maintained a bright line between the board of directors and senior management. Under this governance model, management's role evolved into "telling and selling" strategy and the board's role became to ratify the senior team's vision. Many of the directors we spoke with consider these practices to be outdated; however, navigating new roles for the board and management in setting innovation strategy is proving to be the toughest challenge of all.

Many board members reported a reluctance to ask their most-pressing questions, because they don't want to be perceived as "micromanaging" or "second-guessing management" or as criticizing the CEO in front of his or her team. Meanwhile, several CEOs told us that their boards' arm's-length behavior inhibited the understanding and support required to forge ahead and innovate. When boards do dig into the details of management's innovation proposals, their tough questioning can sometimes be perceived as hostile. Several CEOs experienced such interactions as evaluative of their own performance rather than of the quality of the ideas under discussion, and many complained that the board's responses can be "harsh" or "unfair." In some of our interviews, we could see the emotional toll of these often-heated interactions on the faces of board members and CEOs.

(Re)building the Board for Innovation

The research is clear: Innovation requires passionate discussion, debate, and even conflict—most often among individuals with diverse perspectives. To find better ways of governing innovation, more boards are revisiting both their board composition and the way in which they interact. However, directors are often reluctant to speak publicly—including to us—about how their boards operate, making it hard for boards to share best practices. This is especially problematic when it comes to innovation—an area where directors often feel there is work to be done. Our research revealed four key areas for improvement:

Diversity and collective literacy

When adding or replacing members, boards should take a disciplined approach, seeking members whose expertise complements that of the existing board and, more important, that of management. For example, a director of a traditional operations-focused company reported seeking board members with experience leading exceptional customer-service-oriented companies. Tom Wilson, the CEO of Allstate, pointed out that it was a board member from the manufacturing sector working with OEMs and some of the hot start-ups in the connected car space who was able to offer unique insights into consumer behavior.

In addition, most board members we spoke with wanted more people with technology experience—so-called "digital directors." They believed that directors from organizations reputed to be tech pioneers were likely to be more familiar with the challenges that come with doing innovative work and better prepared to offer informed advice on how to address them. They also wanted directors with the capacity to assess whether or not their companies were investing sufficiently in technology and associated talent.

To further bolster out-of-the-box thinking, a few boards are explicitly including intellectual or problem solving diversity-difficult qualities to assess—in their composition matrices. Most directors we spoke with expressed concerns about whether their board composition was representative of their customers and stakeholders (with regard to factors such as gender, nationality, race, and ethnicity). And a handful of boards are making serious efforts to bring in younger-than-usual candidates, including Millennials, betting on potential rather than experience—a dramatic shift from the traditional approach.

For diverse individuals to collaborate effectively, they need shared experiences and knowledge to serve as a foundation for their interactions and decision making. Forward-thinking companies actively develop the collective literacy and contextual intelligence of the board—cultivating, in particular, a shared set of assumptions about where their industry and markets are going so that they are prepared to make the right risk/reward judgment calls together with management. Nearly half of the directors we spoke with bring in experts from different or adjacent industries to hold "master classes" Some hold sessions with angel investors and venture capitalists to gain their industry insight. Others make visits to technology hubs such as Silicon Valley, accelerators in emerging markets, and companies and academic laboratories working on the cutting edge of a given area. A few told us they meet with key customers in small groups, while others say that their entire boards attend industry conferences together. Directors reported that all these activities prompt important discussions about their appetite for innovation by exposing them to "next practices," not just best practices.

Creative abrasion

This is the ability to develop a marketplace of ideas not from a single flash of insight but from a series of sparks generated through rigorous discourse and debate. Boards today recognize that creative abrasion is a core capability needed to engage in innovative problem-solving. One board member remarked, "Critical thinking is imperative, and that involves putting some friction into [the discussion] to fight the status quo." Another stated, "Sometimes you need to create tension to stimulate thinking, ideas, and innovation."

Indeed, the "mostly silent" board member is no longer seen as doing the job. The outspoken director once perceived as a "gadfly" is now accepted, even welcomed, in the boardroom. Boards need to learn to "tolerate some chaos" in meetings, according to one board member, if they expect management to engage in creative thinking. They must build a culture in which contrarian viewpoints are heard, even actively seeking directors with the "willingness and the dynamism to really mix it up in the boardroom," as one CEO told us.

We weren't surprised to hear that many boards are reluctant to have the frank conversations required for innovation because the dynamics of creative abrasion are so tough to manage. The default for many board members is to avoid conflict and become "too polite." Facilitating creative abrasion is a delicate dance: Boards that are too supportive fail to sufficiently challenge proposals, but too much confrontation can stifle people's willingness to offer ideas.

Redefining the partnership

Balancing the board's legal power and management's executive power is not easy, but for innovation discussions to happen, neither side can dominate. Boards need to build a strong partnership with management and a sense of shared ownership of the innovation strategy. Allstate CEO Tom Wilson told us that unlike most boards, which meet to discuss strategy once a year, his board holds two separate strategy meetings: One is a dialogue about the company's capabilities and market position and is focused on learning; the other is for decision making.

Some CEOs are getting more comfortable using the board as a thought partner. One described his board meetings now as "great idea-sparring sessions," with a healthy degree of conflict and debate. As one of his board members admitted, she had to learn "how to have her nose in, but her fingers out." Understandably, these sessions can be emotionally draining; some CEOs said they felt that their boards sometimes overstepped or "came on too strong." The CEO of a *Fortune* 100 retailer told us, "I've learned from watching other CEOs and boards that if a board gets too far in the weeds, it is deadly." Boards can avoid these issues by clarifying expectations at the outset.

Our research indicates that management teams are increasingly willing to make themselves vulnerable, embracing the board's probing questions about their big-bet ideas and even discussing efforts that didn't pan out. The more courageous CEOs we spoke with said they now seek more input from their board rather than less. One said he encourages dialogue with the board by asking management to share not only recommendations but also the other alternatives that were considered and rejected. Without this transparency, he explained, board members get frustrated and feel as though they are being "sold stuff" by management.

Getting to a place where management teams feel they can bring forward a portfolio of ideas, some of which are more developed than others, requires a real partnership mindset with boards—a shift in the conventional relationship between the two bodies. As former CEO of Mastercard Bob Selander told us, "Some people like to think that one big idea will lead to massive change, yet great boards recognize that it takes ongoing discussions about lots of ideas—the good and the bad—to produce breakthrough results." For one CEO, this meant coaching his executives to expect and be open to hard questions and criticism, acknowledging that it's not easy for his team to expose themselves (and their proposals) to negative reactions from individuals who often have less expertise about the matters at hand. "We had to be very explicit about saying, 'We are not asking for your approval; we are still trying to figure this out,'" another CEO told us. Another said that trust was essential in building a collaborative mindset. "There's a sense now that when we get done with a conversation, neither side feels beat up. Instead we feel like we got to a better decision."

Encouraging risk and living with failure

Boards know their companies must pursue not only incremental improvements but also breakthrough innovation. To foster both kinds of activity, they have to create a culture that is receptive to risk and the inevitable failure that comes with innovative problem solving. However, boards are not—and should not be—interested in innovating for innovation's sake. To avoid innovation activity that doesn't "move the needle," CEOs and board members we spoke with focused on taking risks on efforts that were most likely to create shareholder value in the long term.

Determining whether an innovation at scale will be worth the investment is a very difficult proposition. One board member told us, "Discounted cash flow analyses won't help us make a discussion about a breakthrough idea." This is especially the case in large companies where, as one CEO observed, it is always difficult to make a significant impact on topline growth.

Most board members in our study admit that they struggle with how to weigh shorter-term financial outcomes against other measures—such as customer-experience or market-share metrics, which might be better indicators of whether an innovation will bear fruit and improve the company's competitive position in the long run. Rather than rely on outcome metrics, some boards are beginning to depend more on process measures when evaluating innovation initiatives. For example, one board member said that he frequently asked his team what the company was learning about its customers as it experimented. In some cases, boards also track vitality indices—the percentage of total revenue that comes from new products and services—to measure the organization's innovation capacity as a whole.

We know from a deep body of research that many—even most—innovation efforts fail. So boards must learn to recognize when an initiative should be abandoned. A number of board members said they wanted their companies to figure out how to "fail fast and learn fast" so that they can get on with other endeavors. Some directors said they now make sure to state aloud in board meetings that some innovation efforts should be expected to fail. Although none of the board members we interviewed reported having discussions about the difference between "praiseworthy" and "blameworthy" failures, as Harvard Business School professor Amy Edmondson calls them, they recognize that you can't plan your way to an innovation, you have to act your way there, and that there are bound to be missteps along the way. Indeed, board members say they are wary of CEOs who "play it safe," as one described. A sizable number of the search committee chairs we spoke with said they are skeptical of executive candidates who have never experienced failure and look for potential CEO successors to show, as another director said, "stretch efforts that included missteps and learning from them."

Governing innovation is not for the faint of heart. The journey takes time and determination. It takes the courage to act in the long-term interests of the organization even when markets are more short-sighted. It takes the determination to fight the natural human aversion to risk and the fortitude to engage in creative abrasion.

Balancing power between the board and management has never been easy, but our study suggests that as more boards are embracing new norms, a new contract between boards and management is emerging, making it possible, at last, for directors and CEOs to work together to support and facilitate innovation.

Originally published in November–December 2017. Reprint R1706G

What Amazon's Board Was Getting Wrong About Diversity and Hiring

by Stephanie K. Johnson

Amazon came under fire after its board opposed a shareholder proposal to increase the diversity of the board in May of 2018. (The company responded to blowback by reversing the decision just one week later.) CtW Investment Group, an activist shareholder group, requested that Amazon implement something much like the "Rooney Rule," a requirement instituted by the NFL in 2003 that every team must interview at least one minority candidate for an open head coach or general manager position. In Amazon's case, the proposal required that "the initial list of candidates from which new management-supported director nominees are chosen should include (but need not be limited to) qualified women and minority candidates." At the time, all 10 of the directors on Amazon's board were white, and seven were men.

Companies like Microsoft and Costco use this type of process for their board selection, as increasing diversity of candidate slates is an important step for increasing diversity of the board overall. But Amazon's board recommended voting against the proposal. In its SEC proxy statement to shareholders, the company stated that it already had "complex processes" in place to select board members and that this new requirement would not be a good use of its time or resources. Amazon's communications representative suggested that using a policy like the Rooney Rule was likely to create a "check the box" approach, which is something I've found in previous research.

However, two points are worth mentioning. First, this suggestion misinterprets my findings with coauthors David Hekman and

Elsa Chan in HBR. Our research, which explored status quo bias, or the desire to preserve the current state of things, found that when there is only one woman or person of color in a finalist pool of job candidates, that candidate stands out so much that they have essentially no chance of being hired. This is consistent with the idea that simply interviewing one African American applicant—as required by the Rooney Rule—would not create change. But importantly, we also found that interviewing two women or minority candidates can make the difference and lead to their hiring. So the evidence suggests that mandating diverse candidate slates can improve diversity overall.

This finding holds when we look at the Rooney Rule itself. My colleagues and I researched who was interviewed for the 35 head coaching positions the NFL saw open over the last five years (2013–2017). Of the coaches who have been hired over this period, 29 have been white men and six have been black men.

Most of the time (in 22 instances), only one black coach was interviewed, but in 12 cases two or more black coaches were interviewed. From the 22 times that only one black coach was interviewed, a black coach was only hired once, which is about 5% of the cases. (On average, about five potential coaches are interviewed for each position. So by chance alone, you'd expect a black coach to be hired 20% of the time.) But from the 12 instances where two black coaches were interviewed, a black coach was hired four times (or 33% of the time), which is closer to what you'd expect if each candidate had an equal chance of being selected. These are small numbers; however, the difference between them is statistically significant ($B = 2.35$, $p < .05$, $EXP(B)=10.50$).

There is little doubt that the Rooney Rule brought change to the NFL: It changed the culture and increased awareness about the lack of ethnic diversity at the top of the league. But concerns that progress has been too slow (considering that 70% of players but only 25% of head coaches are African American), can be explained by the fact that interviewing one African American head coach is simply not enough. Our data would argue that if teams were required to interview two African American coaches, that number might increase to 33%.

So when it comes to companies like Amazon that are afraid of "creating token candidates"—individuals who are interviewed to "check a box" but given no real consideration—on finalist slates for board positions, I agree: Interviewing one person of color might not necessarily lead to greater diversity. But the crucial point is that interviewing more than one might—and interviewing all white candidates will obviously not result in hiring a person of color.

The second point worth mentioning is that Amazon's resistance to a formal requirement about diversity isn't unusual. In my work interviewing CEOs of S&P 500 companies (conducted with Kim Davis), I learned that companies are often reluctant to change their board practices due to fear of change and the unknown. It feels much safer to share your greatest corporate secrets with people you already know, which probably explains the strong and consistent data showing that most new board members are recruited from the small, preexisting networks of current board members.

It's been found that CEOs who increased the demographic diversity of their boards elicited higher profit margins for the company, but it came at the expense of lower pay for themselves. And using 12 years of data on Fortune 500 companies, other researchers showed that demographically diverse boards are more likely to challenge the authority of the CEO and curtail CEO pay. A McKinsey study showed that only 14% of C-suite executives select board members on the basis of having a "reputation for independent thinking."

My research found that CEOs who did push for diversity on their boards were very focused on the benefits it would bring, while CEOs who did not tended to focus on the things they would lose (like the current group dynamic) or the risks they would encounter (like that people might think the candidate is a token hire). Psychologists have a theory differentiating between these two perspectives: They have found that a focus on playing to win (what's called a promotion focus) can result in growth and improvement in business outcomes, but a focus on trying to avoid losing (prevention focus) tends to result in stagnation.

So focusing on the potential gains in having a more diverse board—such as diversity of thought, a more comprehensive understanding of the customer base, and reduced groupthink—would seem to encourage CEOs to be more intentional about increasing board diversity. Focusing on the risks, on the other hand, would result in maintaining the status quo—which usually means a board composed of all white members.

The truth is that the status quo is hard to overcome. Selecting a board is kind of like choosing the group of people you want to spend Thanksgiving dinner with—you want to like them and feel comfortable with them. But the magic happens when things are not quite comfortable, when you are hearing different perspectives and being challenged on how you think. Difference of thought and perspective is what makes companies great.

Compared with the other tech companies that have mostly white executives (68% at Apple, 65% at Google), Amazon is among the worst in terms of diversity, with 74% white executives. Of its 18 highest-level executives, 17 are white men. Clearly the company's employees care about increasing diversity in the upper ranks, and Amazon stands to gain by being more representative of the people it serves. Appreciating the need for diversity, and setting some real goals for achieving it at the highest levels, is the only way to ensure that it exists throughout the organization.

Adapted from content originally published on May 14, 2018. Reprint H04BZ2

Managing Risks

A New Framework. *by Robert S. Kaplan and Anette Mikes*

WHEN TONY HAYWARD BECAME CEO OF BP, in 2007, he vowed to make safety his top priority. Among the new rules he instituted were the requirements that all employees use lids on coffee cups while walking and refrain from texting while driving. Three years later, on Hayward's watch, the *Deepwater Horizon* oil rig exploded in the Gulf of Mexico, causing one of the worst man-made disasters in history. A U.S. investigation commission attributed the disaster to management failures that crippled "the ability of individuals involved to identify the risks they faced and to properly evaluate, communicate, and address them."

Hayward's story reflects a common problem. Despite all the rhetoric and money invested in it, risk management is too often treated as a compliance issue that can be solved by drawing up lots of rules and making sure that all employees follow them. Many such rules, of course, are sensible and do reduce some risks that could severely damage a company. But rules-based risk management will not diminish either the likelihood or the impact of a disaster such as *Deepwater Horizon*, just as it did not prevent the failure of many financial institutions during the 2007–2008 credit crisis.

Understanding the three categories of risk

The risks that companies face fall into three categories, each of which requires a different risk-management approach. Preventable risks, arising from within an organization, are monitored and controlled through rules, values, and standard compliance tools. In contrast, strategy risks and external risks require distinct processes that encourage managers to openly discuss risks and find cost-effective ways to reduce the likelihood of risk events or mitigate their consequences.

Category 1: Preventable risks	Category 2: Strategy risks	Category 3: External risks
Risks arising from within the company that generate no strategic benefits	Risks taken for superior strategic returns	External, uncontrollable risks
Risk mitigation objective		
Avoid or eliminate occurrence cost-effectively	Reduce likelihood and impact cost-effectively	Reduce impact cost-effectively should risk event occur
Control model		
Integrated culture-and-compliance model: Develop mission statement; values and belief systems; rules and boundary systems; standard operating procedures; internal controls and internal audit	Interactive discussions about risks to strategic objectives drawing on tools such as: • Maps of likelihood and impact of identified risks • Key risk indicator (KRI) scorecards Resource allocation to mitigate critical risk events	"Envisioning" risks through: • Tail-risk assessments and stress testing • Scenario planning • War-gaming
Role of risk-management staff function		
Coordinates, oversees, and revises specific risk controls with internal audit function	Runs risk workshops and risk review meetings Helps develop portfolio of risk initiatives and their funding Acts as devil's advocates	Runs stress-testing, scenario-planning, and war-gaming exercises with management team Acts as devil's advocates
Relationship of the risk-management function to business units		
Acts as independent overseers	Acts as independent facilitators, independent experts, or embedded experts	Complements strategy team or serves as independent facilitators of "envisioning" exercises

For all the rhetoric about its importance and the money invested in it, risk management is too often treated as a compliance issue.

A rules-based risk-management system may work well to align values and control employee behavior, but it is unsuitable for managing risks inherent in a company's strategic choices or the risks posed by major disruptions or changes in the external environment. Those types of risk require systems aimed at generating discussion and debate.

For strategy risks, companies must tailor approaches to the scope of the risks involved and their rate of change. Though the risk-management functions may vary from company to company, all such efforts must be anchored in corporate strategic-planning processes.

To manage major external risks outside the company's control, companies can call on tools such as war-gaming and scenario analysis. The choice of approach depends on the immediacy of the potential risk's impact and whether it arises from geopolitical, environmental, economic, or competitive changes.

In this article, we present a new categorization of risk that allows executives to tell which risks can be managed through a rules-based model and which require alternative approaches. We examine the individual and organizational challenges inherent in generating open, constructive discussions about managing the risks related to strategic choices and argue that companies need to anchor these discussions in their strategy formulation and implementation processes. We conclude by looking at how organizations can identify and prepare for nonpreventable risks that arise externally to their strategy and operations.

Managing Risk: Rules or Dialogue?

The first step in creating an effective risk-management system is to understand the qualitative distinctions among the types of risks that organizations face. Our field research shows that risks fall into one of three categories. Risk events from any category can be fatal to a company's strategy and even to its survival.

Identifying and Managing Preventable Risks

COMPANIES CANNOT ANTICIPATE EVERY CIRCUMSTANCE or conflict of interest that an employee might encounter.

Thus, the first line of defense against preventable risk events is to provide guidelines clarifying the company's goals and values.

The Mission

A well-crafted mission statement articulates the organization's fundamental purpose, serving as a "true north" for all employees to follow. The first sentence of Johnson & Johnson's renowned credo, for instance, states, "We believe our first responsibility is to the doctors, nurses and patients, to mothers and fathers, and all others who use our products and services," making clear to all employees whose interests should take precedence in any situation. Mission statements should be communicated to and understood by all employees.

The Values

Companies should articulate the values that guide employee behavior toward principal stakeholders, including customers, suppliers, fellow employees, communities, and shareholders. Clear value statements help employees avoid violating the company's standards and putting its reputation and assets at risk.

Category I: Preventable risks

These are internal risks, arising from within the organization, that are controllable and ought to be eliminated or avoided. Examples are the risks from employees' and managers' unauthorized, illegal, unethical, incorrect, or inappropriate actions and the risks from breakdowns in routine operational processes. To be sure, companies should have a zone of tolerance for defects or errors that would not cause severe damage to the enterprise and for which achieving complete avoidance would be too costly. But in general, companies should seek to eliminate these risks since they get no strategic benefits from taking them on. A rogue trader or an employee bribing a local official may produce some short-term profits for the firm, but over time such actions will diminish the company's value.

The Boundaries

A strong corporate culture clarifies what is not allowed. An explicit definition of boundaries is an effective way to control actions. Consider that nine of the Ten Commandments and nine of the first 10 amendments to the U.S. Constitution (commonly known as the Bill of Rights) are written in negative terms. Companies need corporate codes of business conduct that prescribe behaviors relating to conflicts of interest, antitrust issues, trade secrets and confidential information, bribery, discrimination, and harassment.

Of course, clearly articulated statements of mission, values, and boundaries don't in themselves ensure good behavior. To counter the day-to-day pressures of organizational life, top managers must serve as role models and demonstrate that they mean what they say. Companies must institute strong internal control systems, such as the segregation of duties and an active whistle-blowing program, to reduce not only misbehavior but also temptation. A capable and independent internal audit department tasked with continually checking employees' compliance with internal controls and standard operating processes also will deter employees from violating company procedures and policies and can detect violations when they do occur.

This risk category is best managed through active prevention: monitoring operational processes and guiding people's behaviors and decisions toward desired norms. Since considerable literature already exists on the rules-based compliance approach, we refer interested readers to the sidebar "Identifying and Managing Preventable Risks" in lieu of a full discussion of best practices here.

Category II: Strategy risks

A company voluntarily accepts some risk in order to generate superior returns from its strategy. A bank assumes credit risk, for example, when it lends money; many companies take on risks through their research and development activities.

Strategy risks are quite different from preventable risks because they are not inherently undesirable. A strategy with high expected returns generally requires the company to take on significant risks, and managing those risks is a key driver in capturing the potential gains. BP accepted the high risks of drilling several miles below the surface of the Gulf of Mexico because of the high value of the oil and gas it hoped to extract.

Strategy risks cannot be managed through a rules-based control model. Instead, you need a risk-management system designed to reduce the probability that the assumed risks actually materialize and to improve the company's ability to manage or contain the risk events should they occur. Such a system would not stop companies from undertaking risky ventures; to the contrary, it would enable companies to take on higher-risk, higher-reward ventures than could competitors with less effective risk management.

Category III: External risks

Some risks arise from events outside the company and are beyond its influence or control. Sources of these risks include natural and political disasters and major macroeconomic shifts. External risks require yet another approach. Because companies cannot prevent such events from occurring, their management must focus on identification (they tend to be obvious in hindsight) and mitigation of their impact.

Companies should tailor their risk-management processes to these different categories. While a compliance-based approach is effective for managing preventable risks, it is wholly inadequate for strategy risks or external risks, which require a fundamentally different approach based on open and explicit risk discussions. That, however, is easier said than done; extensive behavioral and organizational research has shown that individuals have strong cognitive biases that discourage them from thinking about and discussing risk until it's too late.

Why Risk Is Hard to Talk About

Multiple studies have found that people overestimate their ability to influence events that, in fact, are heavily determined by chance. We tend to be *overconfident* about the accuracy of our forecasts and risk assessments and far too narrow in our assessment of the range of outcomes that may occur.

We also *anchor our estimates* to readily available evidence despite the known danger of making linear extrapolations from recent history to a highly uncertain and variable future. We often compound this problem with a *confirmation bias,* which drives us to favor information that supports our positions (typically successes) and suppress information that contradicts them (typically failures). When events depart from our expectations, we tend to *escalate commitment,* irrationally directing even more resources to our failed course of action—throwing good money after bad.

Organizational biases also inhibit our ability to discuss risk and failure. In particular, teams facing uncertain conditions often engage in *groupthink*: Once a course of action has gathered support within a group, those not yet on board tend to suppress their objections—however valid—and fall in line. Groupthink is especially likely if the team is led by an overbearing or overconfident manager who wants to minimize conflict, delay, and challenges to his or her authority.

Collectively, these individual and organizational biases explain why so many companies overlook or misread ambiguous threats. Rather than mitigating risk, firms actually incubate risk through the *normalization of deviance,* as they learn to tolerate apparently minor failures and defects and treat early warning signals as false alarms rather than alerts to imminent danger.

Effective risk-management processes must counteract those biases. "Risk mitigation is painful, not a natural act for humans to perform," says Gentry Lee, the chief systems engineer at Jet Propulsion Laboratory (JPL), a division of the U.S. National Aeronautics and Space Administration. The rocket scientists on JPL project teams are top graduates from elite universities, many of whom have never experienced failure at school or work. Lee's biggest challenge in establishing a new risk culture at JPL was to get project teams to feel comfortable thinking and talking about what could go wrong with their excellent designs.

Rules about what to do and what not to do won't help here. In fact, they usually have the opposite effect, encouraging a checklist mentality that inhibits challenge and discussion. Managing strategy risks and external risks requires very different approaches. We start by examining how to identify and mitigate strategy risks.

Managing Strategy Risks

Over the past 10 years of study, we've come across three distinct approaches to managing strategy risks. Which model is appropriate for a given firm depends largely on the context in which an organization operates. Each approach requires quite different structures and roles for a risk-management function, but all three encourage employees to challenge existing assumptions and debate risk information. Our finding that "one size does not fit all" runs counter to the efforts of regulatory authorities and professional associations to standardize the function.

Independent experts

Some organizations—particularly those like JPL that push the envelope of technological innovation—face high intrinsic risk as they pursue long, complex, and expensive product-development projects. But since much of the risk arises from coping with known laws of nature, the risk changes slowly over time. For these organizations, risk management can be handled at the project level.

JPL, for example, has established a risk review board made up of independent technical experts whose role is to challenge project engineers' design, risk-assessment, and risk-mitigation decisions. The experts ensure that evaluations of risk take place periodically throughout the product-development cycle. Because the risks are relatively unchanging, the review board needs to meet only once or twice a year, with the project leader and the head of the review board meeting quarterly.

The risk review board meetings are intense, creating what Gentry Lee calls "a culture of intellectual confrontation." As board member Chris Lewicki says, "We tear each other apart, throwing stones and giving very critical commentary about everything that's going on." In the process, project engineers see their work from another perspective. "It lifts their noses away from the grindstone," Lewicki adds.

The meetings, both constructive and confrontational, are not intended to inhibit the project team from pursuing highly ambitious missions and designs. But they force engineers to think in advance about how they will describe and defend their design decisions and whether they have sufficiently considered likely failures and defects. The board members, acting as devil's advocates, counterbalance the engineers' natural overconfidence, helping to avoid escalation of commitment to projects with unacceptable levels of risk.

At JPL, the risk review board not only promotes vigorous debate about project risks but also has authority over budgets. The board establishes cost and time reserves to be set aside for each project component according to its degree of innovativeness. A simple extension from a prior mission would require a 10% to 20% financial reserve, for instance, whereas an entirely new component that had yet to work on Earth—much less on an unexplored planet—could require a 50% to 75% contingency. The reserves ensure that when problems inevitably arise, the project team has access to the money and time needed to resolve them without jeopardizing the launch date. JPL takes the estimates seriously; projects have been deferred or canceled if funds were insufficient to cover recommended reserves.

Facilitators
Many organizations, such as traditional energy and water utilities, operate in stable technological and market environments, with relatively predictable customer demand. In these situations risks stem largely from seemingly unrelated operational choices across a complex organization that accumulate gradually and can remain hidden for a long time.

Since no single staff group has the knowledge to perform operational-level risk management across diverse functions, firms may deploy a relatively small central risk-management group that collects information from operating managers. This increases managers' awareness of the risks that have been taken on across the organization and provides decision makers with a full picture of the company's risk profile.

We observed this model in action at Hydro One, the Canadian electricity company. Chief risk officer John Fraser, with the explicit backing of the CEO, runs dozens of workshops each year at which employees from all levels and functions identify and rank the principal risks they see to the company's strategic objectives. Employees use an anonymous voting technology to rate each risk, on a scale of 1 to 5, in terms of its impact, the likelihood of occurrence, and the strength of existing controls. The rankings are discussed in the workshops, and employees are empowered to voice and debate their risk perceptions. The group ultimately develops a consensus view that gets recorded on a visual risk map, recommends action plans, and designates an "owner" for each major risk.

Hydro One strengthens accountability by linking capital allocation and budgeting decisions to identified risks. The corporate-level capital-planning process allocates hundreds of millions of dollars, principally to projects that reduce risk effectively and efficiently. The risk group draws upon technical experts to challenge line engineers' investment plans and risk assessments and to provide independent expert oversight to the resource allocation process. At the annual capital allocation meeting, line managers have to defend their proposals in front of their peers and top executives. Managers want their projects to attract funding in the risk-based capital planning process, so they learn to overcome their bias to hide or minimize the risks in their areas of accountability.

Embedded experts
The financial services industry poses a unique challenge because of the volatile dynamics of asset markets and the potential impact of decisions made by decentralized traders and investment

managers. An investment bank's risk profile can change dramatically with a single deal or major market movement. For such companies, risk management requires embedded experts within the organization to continuously monitor and influence the business's risk profile, working side by side with the line managers whose activities are generating new ideas, innovation, and risks—and, if all goes well, profits.

JP Morgan Private Bank adopted this model in 2007, at the onset of the global financial crisis. Risk managers, embedded within the line organization, report to both line executives and a centralized, independent risk-management function. The face-to-face contact with line managers enables the market-savvy risk managers to continually ask "what if" questions, challenging the assumptions of portfolio managers and forcing them to look at different scenarios. Risk managers assess how proposed trades affect the risk of the entire investment portfolio, not only under normal circumstances but also under times of extreme stress, when the correlations of returns across different asset classes escalate. "Portfolio managers come to me with three trades, and the [risk] model may say that all three are adding to the same type of risk," explains Gregoriy Zhikarev, a risk manager at JP Morgan. "Nine times out of 10 a manager will say, 'No, that's not what I want to do.' Then we can sit down and redesign the trades."

The chief danger from embedding risk managers within the line organization is that they "go native," aligning themselves with the inner circle of the business unit's leadership team—becoming deal makers rather than deal questioners. Preventing this is the responsibility of the company's senior risk officer and—ultimately—the CEO, who sets the tone for a company's risk culture.

Avoiding the Function Trap

Even if managers have a system that promotes rich discussions about risk, a second cognitive-behavioral trap awaits them. Because many strategy risks (and some external risks) are quite predictable— even familiar—companies tend to label and compartmentalize them, especially along business function lines. Banks often manage what they label "credit risk," "market risk," and "operational risk" in separate groups. Other companies compartmentalize the management of "brand risk," "reputation risk," "supply chain risk," "human resources risk," "IT risk," and "financial risk."

Such organizational silos disperse both information and responsibility for effective risk management. They inhibit discussion of how different risks interact. Good risk discussions must be not only confrontational but also integrative. Businesses can be derailed by a combination of small events that reinforce one another in unanticipated ways.

Managers can develop a companywide risk perspective by anchoring their discussions in strategic planning, the one integrative process that most well-run companies already have. For example, Infosys, the Indian IT services company, generates risk discussions from the Balanced Scorecard, its management tool for strategy measurement and communication. "As we asked ourselves about what risks we should be looking at," says M.D. Ranganath, the chief risk officer, "we gradually zeroed in on risks to business objectives specified in our corporate scorecard."

In building its Balanced Scorecard, Infosys had identified "growing client relationships" as a key objective and selected metrics for measuring progress, such as the number of global clients with annual billings in excess of $50 million and the annual percentage increases in revenues from large clients. In looking at the goal and the performance metrics together, management realized that its strategy had introduced a new risk factor: client default. When Infosys's business was based on numerous small clients, a single client default would not jeopardize the company's strategy. But a default by a $50 million client would present a major setback. Infosys began to monitor the credit default swap rate of every large client as a leading indicator of the likelihood of default. When a client's rate increased, Infosys would accelerate collection of receivables or request progress payments to reduce the likelihood or impact of default.

To take another example, consider Volkswagen do Brasil (subsequently abbreviated as VW), the Brazilian subsidiary of the

German carmaker. VW's risk-management unit uses the company's strategy map as a starting point for its dialogues about risk. For each objective on the map, the group identifies the risk events that could cause VW to fall short of that objective. The team then generates a Risk Event Card for each risk on the map, listing the practical effects of the event on operations, the probability of occurrence, leading indicators, and potential actions for mitigation. It also identifies who has primary accountability for managing the risk. (See the exhibit "The Risk Event Card.") The risk team then presents a high-level summary of results to senior management. (See "The Risk Report Card.")

Beyond introducing a systematic process for identifying and mitigating strategy risks, companies also need a risk oversight structure. Infosys uses a dual structure: a central risk team that identifies general strategy risks and establishes central policy, and specialized functional teams that design and monitor policies and controls in consultation with local business teams. The decentralized teams have the authority and expertise to help the business lines respond to threats and changes in their risk profiles, escalating only the exceptions to the central risk team for review. For example, if a client relationship manager wants to give a longer credit period to a company whose credit risk parameters are high, the functional risk manager can send the case to the central team for review.

These examples show that the size and scope of the risk function are not dictated by the size of the organization. Hydro One, a large company, has a relatively small risk group to generate risk awareness and communication throughout the firm and to advise the executive team on risk-based resource allocations. By contrast, relatively small companies or units, such as JPL or JP Morgan Private Bank, need multiple project-level review boards or teams of embedded risk managers to apply domain expertise to assess the risk of business decisions. And Infosys, a large company with broad operational and strategic scope, requires a strong centralized risk-management function as well as dispersed risk managers who support local business decisions and facilitate the exchange of information with the centralized risk group.

The Risk Event Card

VW do Brasil uses Risk Event Cards to assess its strategy risks. First, managers document the risks associated with achieving each of the company's strategic objectives. For each identified risk, managers create a risk card that lists the practical effects of the event's occurring on operations. Below is a sample card looking at the effects of an interruption in deliveries, which could jeopardize VW's strategic objective of achieving a smoothly functioning supply chain.

Strategic objective	Risk event	Outcomes	Risk indicators	Likelihood/ Consequences	Management controls	Accountable manager
Guarantee reliable and competitive supplier-to-manufacturer processes	Interruption of deliveries	Overtime	Critical items report		Hold daily supply chain meeting with logistics, purchasing, and QA	Mr. O. Manuel, director of manufacturing logistics
		Emergency freight	Late deliveries			
		Quality problems	Incoming defects		Monitor suppliers' tooling to detect deterioration	
		Production losses	Incorrect component shipments		Risk mitigation initiative: Upgrade suppliers' tooling	
					Risk mitigation initiative: Identify the key supply chain executive at each critical supplier	

The Risk Report Card

VW do Brasil summarizes its strategy risks on a Risk Report Card organized by strategic objectives (excerpt below). Managers can see at a glance how many of the identified risks for each objective are critical and require attention or mitigation. For instance, VW identified 11 risks associated with achieving the goal "Satisfy the customer's expectations." Four of the risks were critical, but that was an improvement over the previous quarter's assessment. Managers can also monitor progress on risk management across the company.

Strategic objective	Assessed risks	Critical risks	Trend
Achieve market share growth	4	1	↔
Satisfy the customer's expectations	11	4	↑
Improve company image	13	1	↔
Develop dealer organization	4	2	↔
Guarantee customer-oriented innovations management	5	2	↓
Achieve launch management efficiency	1	0	↔
Increase direct processes efficiency	4	1	↔
Create and manage a robust production volume strategy	2	1	↓
Guarantee reliable and competitive supplier-to-manufacturer processes	9	3	↔
Develop an attractive and innovative product portfolio	4	2	↓

Managing the Uncontrollable

External risks, the third category of risk, cannot typically be reduced or avoided through the approaches used for managing preventable and strategy risks. External risks lie largely outside the company's control; companies should focus on identifying them, assessing their potential impact, and figuring out how best to mitigate their effects should they occur.

Some external risk events are sufficiently imminent that managers can manage them as they do their strategy risks. For example, during the economic slowdown after the global financial crisis, Infosys identified a new risk related to its objective of developing a global workforce: an upsurge in protectionism, which could lead to tight restrictions on work visas and permits for foreign nationals in several OECD countries where Infosys had large client engagements. Although protectionist legislation is technically an external risk since it's beyond the company's control, Infosys treated it as a strategy risk and created a Risk Event Card for it, which included a new risk indicator: the number and percentage of its employees with dual citizenships or existing work permits outside India. If this number were to fall owing to staff turnover, Infosys's global strategy might be jeopardized. Infosys therefore put in place recruiting and retention policies that mitigate the consequences of this external risk event.

Most external risk events, however, require a different analytic approach either because their probability of occurrence is very low or because managers find it difficult to envision them during their normal strategy processes. We have identified several different sources of external risks:

- *Natural and economic disasters with immediate impact.* These risks are predictable in a general way, although their timing is usually not (a large earthquake will hit someday in California, but there is no telling exactly where or when). They may be anticipated only by relatively weak signals. Examples include natural disasters such as the 2010 Icelandic volcano eruption that closed European airspace for a week and economic disasters such as the bursting of a major asset price bubble. When these risks occur, their effects are typically drastic and immediate, as we saw in the disruption from the Japanese earthquake and tsunami in 2011.

- *Geopolitical and environmental changes with long-term impact.* These include political shifts such as major policy changes, coups, revolutions, and wars; long-term environmental changes such as global warming; and depletion of critical natural resources such as fresh water.

- *Competitive risks with medium-term impact.* These include the emergence of disruptive technologies (such as the internet, smartphones, and bar codes) and radical strategic moves by industry players (such as the entry of Amazon into book retailing and Apple into the mobile phone and consumer electronics industries).

Companies use different analytic approaches for each of the sources of external risk.

Tail-risk stress tests

Stress-testing helps companies assess major changes in one or two specific variables whose effects would be major and immediate, although the exact timing is not forecastable. Financial services firms use stress tests to assess, for example, how an event such as the tripling of oil prices, a large swing in exchange or interest rates, or the default of a major institution or sovereign country would affect trading positions and investments.

The benefits from stress-testing, however, depend critically on the assumptions—which may themselves be biased—about how much the variable in question will change. The tail-risk stress tests of many banks in 2007–2008, for example, assumed a worst-case scenario in which U.S. housing prices leveled off and remained flat for several periods. Very few companies thought to test what would happen if prices began to decline—an excellent example of the tendency to anchor estimates in recent and readily available data. Most companies extrapolated from recent U.S. housing prices, which had gone several decades without a general decline, to develop overly optimistic market assessments.

Scenario planning

This tool is suited for long-range analysis, typically five to 10 years out. Originally developed at Shell Oil in the 1960s, scenario analysis is a systematic process for defining the plausible boundaries of future states of the world. Participants examine political, economic, technological, social, regulatory, and environmental forces and select some number of drivers—typically four—that would have the biggest impact on the company. Some companies explicitly draw on the expertise in their advisory boards to inform them about significant trends, outside the company's and industry's day-to-day focus, that should be considered in their scenarios.

For each of the selected drivers, participants estimate maximum and minimum anticipated values over five to 10 years. Combining the extreme values for each of four drivers leads to 16 scenarios. About half tend to be implausible and are discarded; participants then assess how their firm's strategy would perform in the remaining scenarios. If managers see that their strategy is contingent on a generally optimistic view, they can modify it to accommodate pessimistic scenarios or develop plans for how they would change their strategy should early indicators show an increasing likelihood of events turning against it.

War-gaming

War-gaming assesses a firm's vulnerability to disruptive technologies or changes in competitors' strategies. In a war-game, the company assigns three or four teams the task of devising plausible near-term strategies or actions that existing or potential competitors might adopt during the next one or two years—a shorter time horizon than that of scenario analysis. The teams then meet to examine how clever competitors could attack the company's strategy. The process helps to overcome the bias of leaders to ignore evidence that runs counter to their current beliefs, including the possibility of actions that competitors might take to disrupt their strategy.

Companies have no influence over the likelihood of risk events identified through methods such as tail-risk testing, scenario planning, and war-gaming. But managers can take specific actions to mitigate their impact. Since moral hazard does not arise for non-preventable events, companies can use insurance or hedging to mitigate some risks, as an airline does when it protects itself against sharp increases in fuel prices by using financial derivatives. Another option is for firms to make investments now to avoid much higher costs later. For instance, a manufacturer with facilities in earthquake-prone areas can increase its construction costs to protect critical facilities against severe quakes. Also, companies exposed to different but comparable risks can cooperate to mitigate them. For example, the IT data centers of a university in North Carolina would be vulnerable to hurricane risk while those of a comparable university on the San Andreas Fault in California would be vulnerable to earthquakes. The likelihood that both disasters would happen on the same day is small enough that the two universities might choose to mitigate their risks by backing up each other's systems every night.

The Leadership Challenge

Managing risk is very different from managing strategy. Risk management focuses on the negative—threats and failures rather than opportunities and successes. It runs exactly counter to the "can do" culture most leadership teams try to foster when implementing strategy. And many leaders have a tendency to discount the future; they're reluctant to spend time and money now to avoid an uncertain future problem that might occur down the road, on someone else's watch. Moreover, mitigating risk typically involves dispersing resources and diversifying investments, just the opposite of the intense focus of a successful strategy. Managers may find it antithetical to their culture to champion processes that identify the risks to the strategies they helped to formulate.

For those reasons, most companies need a separate function to handle strategy- and external-risk management. The risk function's size will vary from company to company, but the group must report directly to the top team. Indeed, nurturing a close relationship with senior leadership will arguably be its most critical task; a company's ability to weather storms depends very much on how seriously executives take their risk-management function when the sun is shining and no clouds are on the horizon.

That was what separated the banks that failed in the financial crisis from those that survived. The failed companies had relegated risk management to a compliance function; their risk managers had limited access to senior management and their boards of directors. Further, executives routinely ignored risk managers' warnings about

Cybersecurity Is a Board Responsibility

by Thomas J. Parenty and Jack J. Domet

OVER THE PAST DECADE the costs and consequences of cyberbreaches have grown alarmingly. The total financial and economic losses from the 2017 WannaCry attack, for instance, were estimated to reach $8 billion. In 2018 Marriott discovered that a breach of its Starwood subsidiary's reservation system had potentially exposed the personal and credit-card information of 500 million guests. Hackers seem to keep getting more effective. But in our experience as consultants to clients across the globe, we've found another reason that companies are so susceptible to threats from hacking: They don't know or understand their critical cyberrisks, because they're too focused on their technological vulnerabilities.

When cybersecurity efforts address only technology, the result is company leaders who are poorly informed and organizations that are poorly protected. Discussions of cyberthreats end up being filled with specialized tech jargon, and senior executives can't participate meaningfully in them. The responsibility for addressing risks then gets relegated entirely to cybersecurity and IT staff, whose attention falls mainly on corporate computer systems. The outcome tends to be a long, ill-prioritized list of mitigation tasks. Since no company has the resources to fix every cybersecurity problem, important threats can go unaddressed.

A more fruitful approach is to adopt the view that cybersecurity should focus more on threats' potential impact on a business's activities. Say you're an executive at a chemical company. Instead of asking what cyberattacks might be possible on your computer systems, ask, How could a cyberattack disrupt your supply chain? Or expose your trade secrets? Or make you fail to meet your contractual obligations? Or cause a threat to humanity? That adjustment might seem minor, but when leaders start with crucial activities, they can better prioritize the development of cyberdefenses.

A CEO we worked with, Richard Lancaster of CLP, Asia's third-largest electricity provider, described the shift in mindset this way: "Initially, we viewed cyberrisks primarily as an IT issue. Over time we realized that what was really vulnerable was our electric grid and generating plants. Now we recognize that cyberrisk is really business risk—and my job as CEO is to manage business risk." With this perspective, responsibility shifts from IT to senior executives and boards, who must take an active role and ensure that cybersecurity teams focus on the right threats.

Because boards represent the fiduciary interests of the company's owners and are charged with adopting a long-term view of the company, we believe that they have the authority and responsibility to oversee efforts to identify cyberrisks. When they do, it makes a material difference: Simply by raising questions about the four elements of cyberthreats, directors can prompt companies to pay more attention to critical risks.

For example, if you're a board member, ask for assurance that the company has identified and documented its most critical business activities, the benefits they provide, and the most significant risks they face. You should also confirm that the company's leaders have participated in this process.

Similarly, you will want assurance that the company has up-to-date inventories of the computer systems those business activities rely on. Though you don't need to review the details of the inventories yourself, at your discretion you may seek your own independent validation of them or instruct senior executives to arrange their own review. You should also confirm that the company has processes and tools for keeping the inventories current and ask for a few examples of updates that prove those processes are in use.

And so on down the line: Directors should press company leaders about whether they understand the types of attacks that could threaten critical business activities, what the possible impact to both the company and its stakeholders might be, and who potential cyberadversaries are and what capabilities and motivations they might have. The company should brief the board regularly on its current cyberrisk posture for each critical business activity.

Source: Adapted from "Sizing Up Your Cyberrisks," *Harvard Business Review*, November–December 2019.

Jack J. Domet is a management expert who focuses on helping multinational corporations adapt to shifts in technology, globalization, and consumerism. He is a cofounder of the cybersecurity firm Archefact Group and a coauthor of *A Leader's Guide to Cybersecurity* (Harvard Business Review Press, 2019).

Thomas J. Parenty is an international cybersecurity expert who has worked at the National Security Agency and advised other organizations across the globe. He is a cofounder of the cybersecurity firm Archefact Group and a coauthor of *A Leader's Guide to Cybersecurity* (Harvard Business Review Press, 2019).

highly leveraged and concentrated positions. By contrast, Goldman Sachs and JPMorgan Chase, two firms that weathered the financial crisis well, had strong internal risk-management functions and leadership teams that understood and managed the companies' multiple risk exposures. Barry Zubrow, chief risk officer at JP Morgan Chase, told us, "I may have the title, but [CEO] Jamie Dimon is the chief risk officer of the company."

Risk management is nonintuitive; it runs counter to many individual and organizational biases. Rules and compliance can mitigate some critical risks but not all of them. Active and cost-effective risk management requires managers to think systematically about the multiple categories of risks they face so that they can institute appropriate processes for each. These processes will neutralize their managerial bias of seeing the world as they would like it to be rather than as it actually is or could possibly become.

Originally published in June 2012. Reprint R1206B

Ending the CEO Succession Crisis

by Ram Charan

WE TALK ABOUT LEADERSHIP as though leaders—like Tolstoy's happy families—are all alike. But CEO leadership should be a subject apart because it is unique in scope and substance and of incomparable importance. CEOs' performance determines the fates of corporations, which collectively influence whole economies. Our standard of living depends upon excellence at the very top.

Who, then, would dispute that CEO selection deserves perpetual front-burner attention from the custodians of a company's welfare? Surely, when time or trauma ushers in change, organizations should be ready with a clear view of current and future needs and with carefully tended pools of candidates.

But they're not. The CEO succession process is broken in North America and is no better in many other parts of the world. Almost half of companies with revenue greater than $500 million have no meaningful CEO succession plan, according to the National Association of Corporate Directors. Even those that have plans aren't happy with them. The Corporate Leadership Council (CLC), a human-resource research organization, surveyed 276 large companies last year and found that only 20% of responding HR executives were satisfied with their top-management succession processes.

That deficiency is simply inexcusable. A CEO or board that has been in place for six or seven years and has not yet provided a pool of qualified candidates, and a robust process for selecting the next leader, is a failure. Everyone talks about emulating such best practitioners as General Electric, but few work very hard at it.

The result of poor succession planning is often poor performance, which translates into higher turnover and corporate instability. As increased transparency, more vocal institutional investors, and more active boards make greater demands, CEO tenures continue to shrink. Booz Allen Hamilton reports that the global average is now just 7.6 years, down from 9.5 years in 1995. And two out of every five new CEOs fail in the first 18 months, as Dan Ciampa cites in his article "Almost Ready" (HBR, January 2005).

The problem isn't just that more CEOs are being replaced. The problem is that, in many cases, CEOs are being replaced *badly*. Too often, new leaders are plucked from the well-worn Rolodexes of a small recruiting oligarchy and appointed by directors who have little experience hiring anyone for a position higher than COO, vice chairman, CFO, or president of a large business unit. Hiring a CEO is simply different.

Coaxing former leaders out of retirement is another popular way to fill the void. Celebrated examples include Harry Stonecipher at Boeing, Bill Stavropoulos of Dow Chemical, and Jamie Houghton at Corning. But most "boomerang CEOs" return for just a couple of years, long enough to restore credibility and put a real succession candidate in place. They are not the long-term solution.

To increase their chances of finding a leader who will serve long and well, companies must do three things. First, they should have available a deep pool of internal candidates kept well stocked by a leadership development process that reaches from the bottom to the top. Second, boards should create, then continually update and refine, a succession plan and have in place a thoughtful process for making decisions about candidates. Finally, directors considering outside candidates should be exacting, informed drivers of the executive search process, leading recruiters rather than being led by them.

In my 35 years advising corporations, I have participated in dozens of CEO selections and have closely monitored numerous executive pipelines. Drawing on that experience, I will in these pages first explain why companies make poor appointments and then suggest what they can instead do to make good ones. Using these guidelines,

Idea in Brief

The CEO succession process is broken. Many companies have no meaningful succession plans, and few of the ones that do are happy with them. CEO tenure is shrinking; in fact, two out of five CEOs fail in their first 18 months.

It isn't just that more CEOs are being replaced; it's that they're being replaced *badly*. The problems extend to every aspect of CEO succession: internal development programs, board supervision, and outside recruitment.

While many organizations do a decent job of nurturing middle managers, few have set up the comprehensive programs needed to find the half-dozen true CEO candidates out of the thousands of leaders in their midst. Even more damaging is the failure of boards to devote enough attention to succession. Search committee members often have no experience hiring CEOs; lacking guidance, they supply either the narrowest or the most general of require-

ments and then fail to vet either the candidates or the recruiters.

The result is that too often new CEOs are plucked from the well-worn Rolodexes of a remarkably small number of recruiters. These candidates may be strong in charisma but may lack critical skills or otherwise be a bad fit with the company. The resulting high turnover is particularly damaging, since outside CEOs often bring in their own teams, can cause the company to lose focus, and are especially costly to be rid of.

Drawing on over 35 years of experience with CEO succession, the author explains how companies can create a deep pool of internal candidates, how boards can consistently align strategy and leadership development, and how directors can get their money's worth from recruiters. Choosing a CEO should be not one decision but an amalgam of thousands of decisions made by many people every day over years.

organizations can ensure that all participants—directors, executive recruiters, and sitting CEOs—perform wisely and appropriately when it comes time to choose their next leader.

The Trouble with Outsiders

When companies lack the culture or the processes to grow their own heirs apparent, they have no choice but to look outside. More than a third (37%) of the *Fortune* 1,000 companies are run by external recruits, according to the public affairs firm Burson-Marsteller. Although global data are harder to come by, the worldwide trend appears to be similar. But external candidates are in most cases a greater risk because directors and top management cannot know them as well as they know their own people.

Outsiders are generally chosen because they can do *a* job—turn around the company or restructure the portfolio. But *the* job is to lead a hugely complex organization over many years through an unpredictable progression of shifting markets and competitive terrains. Unfortunately, the requirements for that larger job are often not well defined by the board, which may be focused on finding a savior.

The results are not surprising. In North America, 55% of outside CEOs who departed in 2003 were forced to resign by their boards, compared with 34% of insiders, Booz Allen reports. In Europe, 70% of departing outsiders got the boot, compared with 55% of insiders. Some outside CEOs are barely around long enough to see their photographs hung in the headquarters lobby. Gil Amelio left Apple 17 months after he arrived from National Semiconductor. Ex-IBMer Richard Thoman was out of the top spot at Xerox after 13 months. David Siegel gave up the wheel at Avis Rent A Car for US Airways but departed two years later.

Even under the best circumstances, CEO selection is something of a batting average: Companies will not hit successfully every time. But two or more consecutive outsider outs can have a devastating effect on employees, partners, and strategic position. New leaders import new teams and management styles. Continuity and momentum collapse, the energy to execute dwindles, and morale plummets as employees obsess about who will get the next pink slip. Rather than focus on the competition, companies starts to look inward. Bad external appointments are also expensive, since even poor performance is rewarded with rich severance packages.

The Trouble with Insiders

On the other hand, sometimes an external candidate exists who is, very simply, the best available choice. A skillful, diligent board may discover an outstanding fit between an outsider and the job at hand.

Lou Gerstner and IBM spring to mind. And boards must remember that just as outsiders are not uniformly bad choices, insiders are not uniformly good ones. In certain situations, internal candidates actually present the greater risk.

Some concerns about insiders, ironically, emerge from their very closeness to the company. For example, as "known quantities," they may sail through a lax due-diligence process. Or their social networks and psychological ties may complicate efforts to change the culture. Some will not have had the right experience or been tested in the right ways. Individuals from functional areas may not be up to the task of leading the entire business. Or a shift in the industry or market landscape may render carefully nurtured skills irrelevant. In some cases, the credibility of the outgoing CEO or management team may be so sullied that only a new broom can sweep the company clean.

What's more, companies that have no ongoing senior management development program (currently more the rule than the exception) will in all probability need to look outside, maybe for as long as the next ten to 20 years. Outside candidates, in other words, should always be an option. But so long as they remain the only option, and boards lack rigor in identifying and assessing them, succession is imperiled.

The Trouble with CEO Development

Many organizations do a decent job nurturing middle managers, but meaningful leadership development stops well below the apex. The problem manifests itself as a dearth of senior managers, for which companies must increasingly shop in other neighborhoods. Almost half of respondents to the CLC survey had hired a third or more of their senior executive teams from outside, but only 22% of those did so because they considered external candidates irresistibly appealing. Rather, 45% of all respondents judged that it would take too long or be too expensive to develop successors internally.

It's easy to understand why they feel that way. Even where strong development programs exist, very few leaders will ever be qualified

The Secret of Session C

LOTS OF PEOPLE KNOW ABOUT SESSION C, General Electric's annual, dialogue-intensive review of how its leadership resources match up with its business direction. But inside Session C is a process that almost no one knows about. It's called "tandem assessment," and it is among GE's most potent tools for evaluating CEO candidates—and for helping those rising stars evaluate themselves.

Every year, GE selects a different set of 20 to 25 leaders who might grow into CEOs or top functional leaders and sits each one down for a three- to four-hour session with two human resource heads from outside the person's own business unit. The HR executives trace the budding leader's progression from early childhood (where he grew up, how his parents influenced his style of thinking, what his early values were) through recent accomplishments. They then conduct an exhaustive fact-finding mission both inside and outside the organization, including 360-degree reviews, massive reference checks, and interviews with bosses, direct reports, customers, and peers. Largely eschewing psychology, tandem assessment concentrates instead on observed, measurable performance within the business.

The product of all this effort is a 15- to 20-page document that charts the high potential's work and development over decades. The report—brimming with accolades but also detailing areas for improvement—goes to the nascent leader, who uses it to improve his or her game. It also goes to the individual's business head, the senior human-resource executive in the person's unit, and to corporate headquarters, where it is avidly perused by GE's chairman, the three vice chairmen, and Bill Conaty, senior vice president for corporate human resources. "I usually wait until the end of the workday to read one of these because it takes an hour or so," says Conaty. "You find out incredibly interesting things about people in this process."

Tandem assessment is so intensive that only those swimming closest to the C-suite headwaters undergo it. But GE also encourages business units to conduct their own miniversions of the exercise.

The process not only hands rising leaders a mirror but also broadens their support network. Using HR executives from outside the subject's business unit ensures objectivity and gives the promising star two new mentors and two new reality checks. "If something pops up during your career that doesn't feel quite right and you want outside calibration," Conaty explains, "you might call one of these individuals and say, 'Hey, look, everybody is telling me great things here, but this just happened. Would you read anything into it?'"

to run the company. *Very few.* A $25 billion corporation with 70,000 employees, for instance, may have 3,000 leaders, perhaps 50 to 100 of whom would qualify for one of the ten jobs just below the top. That same company would be fortunate to field five strong internal candidates for CEO—and two or three is a more realistic number. General Electric had around 225,000 workers in 1993 when Jack Welch identified 20 potential successors; over seven years, he winnowed the number to three. In CEO succession, it takes a ton of ore to produce an ounce of gold.

Furthermore, the window in which to spot CEO talent is narrow. Companies require sufficiently seasoned candidates who can be counted on to hold the top job for ten years or more. That puts the age of accession at between 46 and 52. In my experience, for a candidate to be ready by 46, serious development should start by age 30. Recognizing which five saplings in a 3,000-tree forest are the ones to nurture requires a degree of discernment that most line managers and HR departments lack and few are developing.

Some companies do identify candidates early but then fail to evaluate them properly. Such organizations often turn evaluation over to HR, which may rely excessively on packaged databases of leadership traits developed by researchers in the human behavior field. Those programs compare internal high potentials with generic benchmarks along many dimensions, a process that creates fragmented profiles of some cookie-cutter ideal rather than nuanced, individualized portraits. What's more, most of those dimensions reflect only the personality traits and not the skills required of a CEO.

Nor do many companies properly nurture the candidates they identify. Some misjudge the business's needs and consequently emphasize the wrong talents. Only 24% of organizations the CLC surveyed believe their leadership development efforts are aligned with their strategic goals. And those goals can be a moving target, changing in response to sometimes tectonic shifts in the external environment. The marketplace changes. Technology changes. Employees' skills become obsolete even as they develop. What's more, very few in-house executive education programs are designed to impart the skills and know-how that a CEO needs.

But the larger issue is that true development happens on the job, not in a classroom. Few companies know how to get their best people the experiences that would prepare them for the CEO role or to rigorously evaluate them in the jobs they do perform. Many companies, for example, still equate leadership development with circulating candidates through multiple functions. In the 1970s, that was the rule at AT&T, IBM, and Xerox, companies that produced leaders who went on to become CEOs elsewhere—and in some cases failed.

The problem with that approach is that potential candidates don't stay long enough in one position to live with the consequences of their decisions. In addition, functional leaders learn to lead functions, not whole companies. Faced with external competition, they fall back on their functional expertise. You can mine all possible lessons from a turn as VP of marketing and still be blindsided by a P&L.

The Trouble with Boards

Bob Stemple's short stint as the head of General Motors ended ingloriously in 1992—and so did the accepted wisdom that boards should automatically bless the departing CEO's handpicked successor.

Yet while directors describe CEO succession as one of their most consuming issues, they don't appear consumed by it. In a survey by Mercer Delta and the University of Southern California, 40% of corporate directors called their involvement in CEO succession planning less than optimal. (I would hazard to add that far fewer are satisfied with the *outcome* of their involvement.) Only 21% responded that they were satisfied with their level of participation in developing internal candidates for senior management.

A packed agenda is the chief culprit: Governance and fiduciary duties, in particular, command an outsize share of boards' attention. Mercer Delta asked directors to compare the amount of time they spend now with the amount they spent a year earlier on nine key activities. Large majorities reported devoting more or many more hours to monitoring accounting, Sarbanes-Oxley, risk, and financial performance. They also reported spending less time interacting with and preparing potential CEO successors than on any other activity. Yet boards' work on succession represents probably 80% of the value they deliver. If the choice of CEO successor is superb, all subsequent decisions become easier.

Another huge problem is that the vast majority of search committee members have had no experience working together on a CEO succession. As a result, they seldom coalesce into deep-delving bodies that get to the pith of their companies' fundamental needs. So they end up approaching their search with only the demands of the moment or—worse—the broadest of requirements.

As they audition candidates, directors may be seduced by reputation, particularly if they're considering a Wall Street or media darling. A few aspiring CEOs employ publicists who flog rosy stories to journalists; when those leaders are up for other jobs, their press-bestowed halos follow them. Board members can also be blinded by charisma, by the sheer leaderishness of a candidate. There is nothing intrinsically wrong with charisma, though some criticize it as the sheep's clothing in which hubris lurks. But too often directors become so focused on what candidates are *like* that they don't press hard enough to discover what candidates can and cannot *do*.

For example, one board looking for a new CEO after firing the old one asked for someone who could build a great team and get things done. The recruiter presented such a person—an energetic, focused candidate whose personal qualities quickly won over directors. What the organization really needed was someone who could create a stream of new products and win shelf space from powerful retailers in a volatile marketplace. Unfortunately, the directors never specified those requirements or raised them either during interviews or the background check.

The candidate's upstream-marketing skills were poor to nonexistent. The company's market share declined precipitously, and three years later the CEO was out on his ear. On its second try, the board concentrated so hard on marketing that it ignored execution. The next CEO was a visionary and a marketing genius but was unable to get things done. The company, once first in its market, will probably be sold or stumble into Chapter 11.

Finally, directors too often shunt due diligence onto recruiters. As a result, that process can be quite superficial. One company that left vetting to its recruiter and its investment banker found itself saddled with a leader who botched critical people issues. At a postmortem three years later, directors discovered that at his former company the CEO had routinely punted people problems to the chairman, who had been CEO before him and occupied the office next to his. That would have been nice to know before the pen touched the contract.

The Trouble with Recruiters

Executive recruiters are honest and highly professional. Still, they can wield disproportionate influence in CEO succession decisions. One reason is concentration. Just three recruiters control some 80% of the *Fortune* 100 CEO search market (a single firm claims fully 60% of it), and one or two people within those companies direct the most important searches. These firms' social networks are vast and powerful. Anyone with a smidgen of ambition in the corporate world knows whom they have to know to get ahead.

At the same time, board members' inexperience and consequent inability to precisely define their needs makes recruiters' task difficult. Recruiters must satisfy their clients yet also manage them, helping the search committee to gel so they can extract the criteria they need while keeping requirements broad enough to cast the widest talent net possible.

When committees don't gel, recruiters may step into the vacuum with their own criteria, and directors too often let them. Unfortunately, no executive recruiter can grasp the subtleties of a client's business as well as the client can. In the absence of effective direction, recruiters generally approach each search with a boilerplate of the 20 or so attributes they consider most desirable for any CEO. That formula tends to overemphasize generic qualities like character and vision, as well as team-building, change-management, and relationship skills. Psychology and chemistry are also very important to executive recruiters: Like directors, they may let a personality surplus overshadow a skills deficit.

In one—granted, extreme—case, the longtime CEO of a company with four highly successful businesses and a huge debt level was retiring. The recruiter produced a list of six candidates, pressing one—the head of a very large division at a multinational company—hard on the board. Yet all the recruiter gave the directors was a page-and-a-half description of this candidate's leadership skills; a list of his extensive connections with unions, customers, and government bodies; and an outline of his swift rise through the organization.

A financial performance history for the candidate's division was not included and not publicly available, so a member of the search committee began to dig. He discovered that return on assets under the candidate's supervision was miniscule over the previous five years, even though his division was four times larger than the entire company considering him for CEO. Furthermore, this man had never earned cost of capital in his life. Even so, the recruiter wanted to put him in charge of a business that had certainly done so—and that hoped to rise to the next level.

Fortunately, after much debate, the committee vetoed the recommendation, opting instead for number three on the recruiter's list—the president of another company, who had consistently improved performance and delivered a 20% return on equity. In his first three years, this new CEO took the stock from 24 to 108 in a slow-moving industry. The board was happy. Management was happy. The recruiter's preferred candidate was happy when he was placed at another, larger company—but then he was fired in six months.

Executive recruiters also succumb to the usual-suspects bias, primarily looking for new heads above other companies' necks. It is just plain easier to compile a list of sitting CEOs than to make a case for—or take a risk on—a COO or an executive VP. Some recruiters go so far as to approach sitting CEOs, even with no specific jobs to dangle, and urge them to consider looking elsewhere. The recruiters' goal is to loosen a prized gem from its setting and thereby beat a fellow recruiter to the punch.

Sometimes, the board's selection of recruiter is flawed from the start. A director may jump the gun, recommending a recruiter he has worked well with even before the search committee is formed. Nor do most boards examine search firms' track records—that is, how many of the CEOs the firm has placed have succeeded and how many have failed. Even if directors did ask that question, they're not likely to get the answer because it appears no one is monitoring recruiters' performance. The stock-buying public, by contrast, knows exactly how well directors score on their CEO choices.

How to Succeed at Succession

Charlie Bell's ascension to the top spot at McDonald's within hours of Jim Cantalupo's death reflected well on a company that had its house in order, particularly when compared—as it inevitably was—with Coca-Cola's simultaneous travails. Similarly, NBC's early, orderly announcement that Brian Williams would replace network news anchor Tom Brokaw stands in stark relief to CBS's public uncertainty over Dan Rather's successor. (Anchors are not CEOs, of course, but they are even more visible and arguably as consequential to their organizations' fortunes.)

By now it should be clear that the most important thing companies can do to improve succession is to bolster their leadership development and focus on those very rare people in their ranks who might one day be CEO. Organizations must identify high-potential candidates early in their careers, and global companies must look in all the countries where they operate. As candidates enter the development pipeline, managers must constantly align their charges' education and on-the-job experience with the emerging landscape. And they must rigorously assess the candidates' performance at each developmental stage.

The very best preparation for CEOs is progression through positions with responsibility for steadily larger and more complex P&L centers. A candidate might start by managing a single product, then a customer segment, then a country, then several product lines, then a business unit, and then a division. Whatever the progression, P&L responsibility at every level is key. The Thomson Corporation, a global provider of information solutions, comprises more than 100 P&Ls, so its top people have abundant opportunity to run a $50 million to $100 million business. "That's the best crucible for formulating leaders that I know of," says Jim Smith, executive vice president of human resources and administration.

Companies not set up to provide such opportunities should create jobs—large projects or small internal organizations—that exercise the P&L muscle. Otherwise, they risk elevating an internal candidate who is not prepared. For example, one $10 billion company in a highly capital-intensive and unionized industry has targeted as CEO successor the head of its smallest division. The candidate is a brilliant, articulate young man but has no experience running a big business in general or this type of business in particular (his own division is knowledge intensive, and unionized labor has no presence). The board is considering creating a deputy position within its largest division for this person and making the 59-year-old current division head (who will retire in three years) his coach, granting that coach a bonus if he ensures his successor's success.

Companies with inflexible functional structures will probably be forced to import P&L-tested leaders from outside and place them in very high positions. To reduce the risk, they should bring in such executives three or four years before the expected succession. That can be challenging, however, because many will demand appointment to the top spot in less than a year.

But leadership development is just part of the solution. Boards, too, can greatly improve the chances of finding a strong successor by acting vigilantly before and during the search. Senior executive development should be overseen by the board's compensation and organization committee, which needs to receive periodic reports on the entire pool of potential CEOs and regular updates on those bobbing near the top of it. The committee should spend a third of its time examining lists of the top 20 candidates in the leadership pipeline. In addition, at least 15% of the 60 or so hours that members meet as a full board should be devoted to succession. At minimum, the board ought to dedicate two sessions a year to hashing over at least five CEO candidates, both internal and external.

And directors should personally get to know the company's rising stars. Promising leaders should be invited to board meetings and to the dinners that precede board meetings, and members should talk with them informally whenever possible. Directors should also meet with and observe candidates within the natural habitats of their business operations. In this way, when it comes time to single out CEO candidates, directors will be considering a set of very well-known quantities.

The "Fit" Imperative

The goal of all these interactions and deliberations is for board members to reach a highly refined but dynamic understanding of the CEO position and their options for it long before appointing a successor. Company leaders should be as well defined as puzzle pieces; their strengths and experiences must match the shape of their organizations' needs. That is, they simply must *fit*. Boards achieve fit by specifying, in terms as precise as possible, three or four aspects of talent, know-how, and experience that are nonnegotiable.

Ideally, these attributes pertain to the organization's dominant needs for the next several years, but they should also relate to future growth. In one recent CEO succession, the company, in conjunction with a boutique recruiting firm, began with impossibly broad criteria that included everything from industry leader to change agent. The process floundered until the search committee narrowed its focus to three qualities: experience in segmenting markets according to customer needs; the talent to grow the business organically; and a track record of building strong executive teams. Those three skills, in addition to general leadership traits, delineated the pond in which this company fished.

The job of defining such qualities belongs to the search committee, which should form well before succession is scheduled to take place. As they wrestle with requirements, committee members must constantly keep in mind the company's changing circumstances, so that an understanding of what currently works doesn't congeal into what works, period.

For example, Bank of America flourished under deal maker par excellence Hugh McColl, Jr., for years. But by the time he stepped down in 2001, integration, rather than acquisition, had become the dominant challenge. Having recognized the altered environment several years before, BOA's board chose not a leader in McColl's image but instead Ken Lewis, a company veteran proficient at integration of acquisitions and organic growth. (For an example of how a company integrates its leadership development with its strategy, see the sidebar "The Living Succession Tree.")

Specific, nonnegotiable criteria also let directors keep control when they work with executive recruiters. With good direction, search firms can be a valuable source of objectivity—benchmarking internal candidates against outsiders and making sure that board members consider all possibilities, even if they prefer an insider. Some companies even bring in recruiters to do independent assessments of insider candidates. Their concurrence with a board's judgment carries weight with shareholders and potential critics.

Search firms ask boards to recommend candidates, and they take those recommendations seriously. But, ultimately, it is the recruiter who compiles the list, and the compiler of the list wields considerable influence. Directors must require from recruiters detailed explanations of how the candidates fulfill their criteria. A ten-page report on each is reasonable.

When the time comes to select the new CEO, directors—ordinarily a polite breed, unaccustomed to challenging one another or asking discomforting questions—must engage in a vigorous discussion of the candidates' comparative merits. One search committee that did an outstanding job making the final decision invited five candidates (two internal and three external) to a hotel for a couple of days. The two internal candidates were favorites of two different directors. On the first day, the committee interviewed three candidates, two external and one internal. The directors split into two groups of three, and each group spoke with one candidate for 90 minutes. After these interviews, the directors broke for 45 minutes to share impressions, then switched candidates. Then the two groups of directors took turns interviewing the third candidate, similarly

The Living Succession Tree

FOUR YEARS AGO, TOP MANAGEMENT at the Thomson Corporation realized that its CEO succession process had passed out of life and into a stagnant existence on paper. Leadership development chugged along separately from business planning. Human resource groups produced reams of documents and charts dense with the branches of succession trees. "We never used them," says Jim Smith, executive vice president of human resources and administration at the $7 billion global company. "I never saw anybody go to a chart and say, 'Let's look at this.'"

So the company decided to rethink talent management in order to field leaders who could run Thomson under whatever conditions might exist. The new process is built on two principles: Succession planning should happen in lockstep with strategy making, and the current CEO should be intimately and visibly involved.

Each February, Thomson's 200 top managers gather to review corporate initiatives. Then in April, CEO Richard Harrington, CFO Robert Daleo, and Smith conduct strategy reviews with emerging leaders in every business unit. Goals coming out of those talks—related to markets, customers, products, and growth areas—accompany the trio into the next round of discussions, which takes place in June and focuses on management development.

At that point, Harrington, Daleo, and Smith devote eight full days to listening to senior executives (including CEO candidates) report on *their* highest

sharing impressions informally. At the end of the first day, the committee members debated over dinner, and the director who had originally advocated for the internal candidate volunteered that he was indeed not the strongest choice. The next day, they repeated the process with the two other candidates, and the results were remarkably the same, with the director who had originally advocated for the internal candidate changing his mind. In the course of these discussions, all hidden agendas fell away, requirements were honed, and directors were able to reach consensus.

Finally, board members must do due diligence on outside candidates—and do it well. Directors must seek reliable external sources and demand candor from them. Board members should ask first about the candidate's natural talents. If those gifts—admirable as they may be—do not match the position's specific profile, that potentials. The trio insists on concrete examples throughout. "It's so easy to generalize on how somebody's doing: 'He's a good guy' and 'She's terrific with people,'" says Smith. "We want to pin down the facts beneath that. 'You say she's good with people. Give me some examples of who she's developed. How many have been promoted?'"

The same people who attended the strategy meetings attend the leadership development meetings, so everyone in the room understands what talent the business requires. And when those same people reconvene again a few months later to discuss budgets, conclusions from the strategy and leadership development rounds inform their decisions. By year's end, Thomson has tightly integrated strategy, leadership, and budget plans. And Harrington and his senior team have spent many, many hours getting to know the company's most-promising CEO candidates.

Smith has three recommendations for companies interested in crafting a similar system, which has proved constructive to managers and the board alike. First, make sure the CEO devotes considerable personal time to identifying, getting to know, and developing leaders. Second, treat leadership development as part of the process used to run the business. And finally, make the process informal enough to encourage conversation. "We used to produce books," says Smith. "Now we have conversations."

candidate is not worth pursuing. Needless to say, due diligence is also the time to root out any fatal character flaws.

At this point, the role of the outgoing CEO is chiefly consultative. He or she must be active in spotting and grooming talent, help define the job's requirements, provide accurate information about both internal and external candidates, and facilitate discussions between candidates and directors. But when the choice of successor is imminent, make no mistake: That decision belongs to the board.

Inside a Development Engine

Despite the current crisis, we know it is possible to build organizations that reliably produce great CEOs. Starting after World War II, a few corporations emerged as veritable leadership factories. Companies like General Electric, Emerson Electric, Sherwin-Williams, Procter & Gamble, and Johnson & Johnson managed to stock not only their own corner offices but also many others. (Of course even great companies sometimes stumble: Procter & Gamble had a failure from within when it promoted Durk Jager to the top spot. But it is going great guns under the stewardship of company veteran A.G. Lafley.)

Reuben Mark has sat atop Colgate-Palmolive for 20 years, so the company's CEO succession chops have not been recently proven. But I believe the consumer products giant has a first-rate process for identifying and developing CEO talent. At the very least it produced three internal candidates who are excellent prospects for the job.

Colgate-Palmolive does business in more than 200 countries, and its emerging leaders are correspondingly international and diverse. Leadership evaluation begins during the first year of employment. "It may seem strange to talk about someone who's been here just a year when discussing the pipeline to the CEO," says Bob Joy, senior vice president of global human resources. "But the earlier you start to identify talent, the earlier you can provide the job assignments and develop the broad business experience needed by a CEO candidate."

Each subsidiary identifies its own high potentials and submits that list to local general managers, who add and subtract names and then hand the list off to the division heads. These lists wend their way up the chain until they reach the Colgate-Palmolive Human Resource (CPHR) committee, composed of Colgate's CEO, president, COO, the senior VP of HR, and the senior candidates up for the top job. CPHR modifies and consolidates the lists into a single master list, dispatching it back down the ranks where managers can contest decisions made by those above them. The process takes place once a year.

Those who make the cut are deployed in one of three tracks. The first track, local talent, is for relatively junior staff who might become the direct reports of a general manager. Someone more advanced would be designated regional talent, and given, for example, a significant position in Asia. The most elevated track—global talent—is the reservoir from which the most senior jobs are filled.

Throughout their careers, all these high potentials receive assignments that stretch their abilities and expand their knowledge, exposing them to a variety of markets, cultures, consumers, and business circumstances. CPHR itself designs career paths for general managers and higher positions because the committee is at the same time dynamically developing the profile of Colgate's future leadership team. (Also, says Joy, "you can imagine the kind of resistance you'd get from a division president who would like to keep his high-potential people in his own area.") The thousand or so highest high potentials (out of a total pool of about 2,000) receive outside executive coaching, which includes 360-degree feedback on current and past assignments.

Having identified its high potentials, Colgate strives to bolster their connection to the company. One tactic is recognition: "If you're talking about the future leaders of your company, you want them to feel special," says Joy. "You want them to have Colgate in their veins." Toward that end, the company sponsors a series of "visibility programs." One, for example, gathers high potentials from all over the world at Colgate's New York headquarters for week-long sessions during which they meet with every senior leader in the company. In addition, each high potential receives a special stock grant, which arrives with a personal letter from the CEO.

Colgate's global growth program mandates that all senior managers retain 90% of their high potentials or lose some compensation. If a high potential at any level, anywhere in the world, does resign, the CEO, the COO, the president, and Joy are alerted within 24 hours and move immediately to retain that person.

Perhaps most important, Joy collaborates with the office of the chairman to connect directors early and often with high potentials in all areas. At the most senior level, functional leaders introduce the board to the top two or three most-promising heirs for their own positions, adding detailed analyses of those candidates' strengths and weaknesses. Emerging leaders routinely take part in presentations to the board and meet informally with directors over lunch. Board members closely track the progress not of one or two people but of the top 200, frequently discussing how each

The Four Kinds of Leadership Judgment: A Framework for Selecting a CEO

by Noel Tichy and Warren Bennis

ULTIMATELY, THE CHOICE OF A CEO is a calculated bet on how good that leader's judgment will be when it comes to selecting the right people, setting the organization's direction, and handling the inevitable crises all organizations face. With Warren Bennis, I have developed a framework that will help in examining a leader's past judgment calls and predicting future calls. The framework identifies four levels of leadership intelligence: judgment about yourself; judgment about your immediate team; judgment about your organization; and judgment related to stakeholders (decisions that involve your board, suppliers, customers, and community). Good leaders need capabilities at all four levels. The chart to the right presents the core issues—regarding people, strategy, and crises—in each area for which leaders must exercise judgment.

Great leaders are defined as such because a high percentage of their judgment calls are good. The key to such high performance is possessing knowledge that goes beyond a "just the facts" analytical capability. It is possessing deeper knowledge of the four domains.

Personal Judgment

- **People:** Personal judgments about your ambitions, role, and capabilities
- **Strategy:** Personal judgments regarding your career and life strategy
- **Crisis:** Personal judgments made during times of crisis and introspection

Team Judgment

- **People:** Judgments about who is on and off your team
- **Strategy:** Judgments about how your team evolves to meet business demands

piece fits into the puzzle and what experiences or skills might improve that fit.

As a result, when CEO succession looms, the board and top management will be able to select from candidates they have spent many, many years observing and evaluating. "If you start five years

- **Crisis:** Judgments about how your team operates and with whom during a crisis

Organizational Judgment

- **People:** Judgments about organizational systems for ensuring quality and capability of people in the organization

- **Strategy:** Judgments about how to engage and align all organizational levels in strategy execution

- **Crisis:** Judgments about how to work with the organization through times of crisis

Stakeholder Judgment

- **People:** Judgments about which stakeholders are important and how to engage them

- **Strategy:** Judgments about engaging stakeholders to frame, define, and execute strategy

- **Crisis:** Judgments about dealing with key stakeholders during times of crisis

Source: *Judgment*, by Noel M. Tichy and Warren G. Bennis (Portfolio, 2007). Excerpted from the article, "The Art and Science of Finding the Right CEO," *Harvard Business Review*, October 2011.

Noel Tichy is a professor of organizational behavior and human resource management at the Ross School of Business at the University of Michigan.

Warren Bennis is a Distinguished Professor of Management at the University of Southern California and the author of *Still Surprised: A Memoir of a Life in Leadership*, with Patricia Ward Biederman (Jossey-Bass, 2010).

or even ten years before the CEO is going to retire," says Joy, "it may be too late."

Of course Colgate-Palmolive—like General Electric—tackles succession from a position of strength. Its CEO has been two decades in the saddle, and he is passionate on the subject of an heir. Companies with less-veteran chiefs—and whose boards have been negligent in this area—will probably need to line up candidates quickly, while laying a deeper pipeline. They will in all likelihood have to bring in outsiders and position them to gain the requisite business and industry experience. That may mean shaking up the leadership team and reporting structures to free up slots in which outsiders can be tested. This restructuring will probably be resented, but it is necessary pain.

A quick infusion of talent may be a company's only course, but it is no way to run a railroad. Organizations without meaningful pipelines must start now to put them in place. Young companies should create the processes that will come to fruition in five or ten years' time. Choosing the CEO's successor is not one decision but the amalgam of thousands of decisions made by many people every day over years and years. Such meticulous, steady attention to defining needs and evaluating candidates produces strong leaders and inspires succession planners at lower levels to exercise the same discipline.

The trend of CEO failures must be reversed. CEO succession is all boards' paramount responsibility; nothing else so profoundly affects their companies' futures. Directors must start investing their time and energy today. The call for a new leader could come tomorrow.

Originally published in February 2005. Reprint R0502C

After the Handshake

by Dan Ciampa

THE MOOD INSIDE THE BOARDROOM was celebratory. For months the directors of this multibillion-dollar industrial and consumer-goods company had been searching for a successor to their longtime CEO. After interviewing multiple candidates, they'd unanimously voted to make an offer. The outside recruit—let's call him Harry—had an exceptional record of growing sales while running a large division of a multinational known as a training ground for world-class CEOs. In interviews he was polished and poised. He asked insightful questions about the company's strategy, raising issues the board hadn't considered previously. His references were effusive. To the directors' delight, Harry, who was simultaneously in the running for two other CEO jobs, accepted their offer—largely because he felt that this company offered the most autonomy and upside. The board announced the appointment at the annual meeting, in April; shortly afterward, the outgoing CEO departed, and Harry started. The directors congratulated themselves on a job well done. The arduous work of succession—their most important duty—was complete.

Except it wasn't, because the board, the outgoing CEO, and the chief human resources officer hadn't laid the groundwork for Harry to succeed. They hadn't discussed with him how decisions were made, how innovation took place, or who had the most influence in the company. As a result, in his first weeks on the job, the new leader was not prepared as he got acquainted with the people he'd inherited and learned the political dynamics of the senior group. For one thing, the CFO was bitterly disappointed at having been passed over for the CEO job and had a reputation for being conniving and power-hungry. For another, although Harry did his best to understand the corporate culture, he failed to fully appreciate the strength of the company's bias toward cost control and its resistance to change. Crucially, in the three months before his first board meeting, in late June, no directors bothered to meet with the new CEO—and he, preferring to keep his own counsel, didn't reach out to them either. "Some of us thought he was so good that there wouldn't be anything we could add," one director recalls. "The net result was that we all decided we should get out of his way."

When, at that first board meeting, Harry laid out an aggressive new strategy—which included combining two divisions and taking on debt to make an acquisition—the directors were taken aback. They'd hired him to drive growth, but they'd expected an evolutionary, incremental approach rather than a rapid, expensive overhaul. They resisted, frustrating the CEO. Over the following months, the CFO's backchannel communications with key directors eroded their confidence in Harry. Fifteen months after signing him, the board forced its star hire to resign—and the company's stock dropped sharply at the news.

A Shared Responsibility

Whether new CEOs are hired from the outside or promoted from within, they should be aware of a daunting statistic: One-third to one-half of new chief executives fail within their first 18 months, according to some estimates. Some of these flameouts can be attributed to poor strategic choices by the new leader, and some result when the board makes an imperfect choice—overestimating a candidate's abilities and potential or hiring a leader whose skill set doesn't fit the context. Sometimes the new leader is obviously responsible for a handoff gone wrong, and other times the board is rightly blamed. But a close look shows that it's rarely that simple. When a succession fails, the responsibility is almost always shared.

Idea in Brief

The Problem

One-third to one-half of new CEOs, whether they're hired from outside or from within, fail within their first 18 months, according to some estimates.

Why It Occurs

Newcomers misread the political situation or overestimate the organization's willingness to abandon old behaviors. Meanwhile, boards and key executives fail to grasp the complex nature of CEO succession or set one-dimensional expectations of the new leader.

What Can Be Done

A comprehensive succession process begins when a candidate accepts the position and lasts for several months after his or her arrival. The outgoing CEO, the chief human resources officer, and the board should all have roles in helping the newcomer navigate company culture and politics.

Whether coming in directly as CEO or into the number two spot expecting to move up, failing newcomers make these common mistakes:

- They don't read the political situation well enough to build necessary relationships and coalitions.

- They don't achieve the cultural changes their strategic and operational agendas require.

- They overestimate the willingness or the capacity of the people they inherit to abandon old habits and behaviors.

Meanwhile, boards and key executives typically:

- Fail to grasp the complex nature of succession and assume that CEO handoffs are as simple as those at lower levels.

- Fail to carefully consider the cultural and political aspects of the company that will be problematic for the new leader in his early months.

- Set one-dimensional or generic expectations of the new leader—in particular, emphasizing only financial and operational goals and not including equally specific cultural, political, and personal ones.

The purpose of a comprehensive approach to transitioning a CEO is to avoid those mistakes. When the transition is done well, the company is prepared for a new leader with a change agenda, and the new leader is more tuned in to power dynamics and how the culture will influence a strategy shift or what cultural changes will be necessary to support it. The transition establishes a solid path toward productive relationships between the CEO and key stakeholders—including, most crucially, board members.

In the United States, presidential candidates typically name a transition team and begin planning for a new administration months before a single vote is cast on Election Day, because they want to be prepared in the event they win. In corporate life, however, too many CEO transitions are informal or improvised. In a 2010 survey conducted by the executive search firm Heidrick & Struggles and Stanford's Rock Center for Corporate Governance, half the companies surveyed reported providing no formal transition plan for a new leader. James Citrin, who leads the North American CEO practice at the recruiting firm Spencer Stuart, estimates that of the companies that do have a transition process, fewer than 20% extend it beyond the new CEO's first week.

A CEO transition is *not* the same as onboarding, which is a formal, short-term, agenda-driven orientation program of briefings and meetings. An onboarding plan can be a useful component of the transition process, just as the formal events at a college's freshman orientation can provide valuable information to new students. But like a college student's assimilation, which takes place slowly and informally (the most valuable moments often occur in dorms and dining halls), a CEO's transition is a longer process of interactions both formal and informal, planned and impromptu. Handled correctly, the process will begin when the board's choice accepts the position and will last for months after she arrives.

The transition is also properly viewed as the second part of a comprehensive succession. Although many people tend to think of succession as the process of identifying and assessing internal and external candidates, defining the characteristics the next CEO will need, and ultimately settling on a final choice, that's really only half the job. Succession should include activities that occur after the new CEO takes the job—activities designed to maximize her chances of success. In many ways, the later stages are more difficult than the recruitment and assessment phases. They involve emotions, ego, beliefs about what the organization should become, and, in particular, company culture and politics. Declaring victory too soon can leave a leader ill equipped to build a base of support. That increases the odds of a succession failure, the costs of which can be substantial—for shareholders, for employees, and for individual careers.

The Three Variables

In the creation and implementation of a comprehensive CEO transition process, three key variables affect structure and timing. First, is the new CEO from inside or outside the company? Second, will he take on that role immediately or spend time as a "designated successor," working alongside the outgoing CEO while typically carrying the title of president or chief operating officer? Third, whether or not the transfer of power is immediate, will the outgoing CEO continue to be a presence in the company, as chairman of the board or as an adviser?

Many companies skimp on or forgo a transition program for an internal candidate who's promoted to CEO. On the surface that makes sense: An internal candidate has already navigated a career with the company, so onboarding may seem superfluous. However, even an internal candidate will benefit from a transition program that recognizes several specific challenges to be faced in the new job. For example, most people promoted from inside have never been a CEO before and must learn to handle a level of responsibility for which they have had little preparation. Furthermore, they will inherit a team made up of former peers, some of whom may have been rivals for the top job, and will benefit from assistance in dealing with that dynamic. And insider CEOs need to forge new relationships with directors, because reporting to and managing a board is vastly different from making periodic presentations to it.

The Role of the Outgoing CEO

In some cases the outgoing CEO plays no role in succession—such as when she has been fired or pushed out. But in a planned succession (which typically involves a retirement), the outgoing CEO can help the incoming one adjust to and understand the company. Not every new leader appreciates having his predecessor stay on for an extended period, but according to a 2012 study by Patrick Wright, of the University of South Carolina, 40% of departing CEOs remain involved with the company (usually as board members or advisers) after giving up the title.

An incumbent CEO plays a particularly important role if the successor joined the organization as an heir apparent. Such an extended transition should begin with defining the roles the two will play. The successor must have substantive responsibilities, objectives closely tied to strategic and operational success, a platform for proving his abilities, and a clear sense of the timetable for ascending to the top job. The two leaders will need to agree on the details of their relationship: On what issues will they collaborate? Do they want the board and the senior team to view them as true partners? Which decisions will the incumbent run by the successor before making them? What milestones or phases will mark their progress, and will the transition of power and responsibility be incremental or all at once?

In these situations, incumbent CEOs direct the transition process. They must remain fully engaged with their current duties and responsible for short-term performance, but they should also devote significant time to ensuring their eventual replacements' early success.

Consider one CEO of a multinational conglomerate who excelled in this role. After 10 years as chairman and CEO, this executive—let's call him Bob—prepared to pass the role to his successor, Greg, who'd been a direct report and headed up the company's largest unit. Like the best successions, this one was planned well in advance: Two years before he intended to retire, Bob led the board through a careful process of defining what characteristics the next CEO would need, assessing potential internal candidates, and examining external options. Once Greg emerged as the board's choice, Bob took ownership of helping him transition into the CEO role.

Unlike many departing CEOs, Bob created a feeling in his executive team that every member had some responsibility for the transition. He assigned each subordinate specific tasks to help Greg prepare, and he made a list of tasks and assignments for himself, too. He analyzed his network of critical relationships and systematically introduced Greg to key contacts. He prepared detailed briefings on how he had made decisions involving regulatory issues, markets, talent, finances, and so on. He offered comprehensive and insightful thoughts on self-management: how he had spent his time, dealt with conflicting requests, managed the administrative system that supported him, kept his energy up, and countered stress. He outlined the strengths and weaknesses of the current executive team and described how he'd tried to reduce tension and conflict among its members. The two men spent hours alone discussing these issues and traveled together to meet customers, regulators, and alliance partners.

Throughout the process, Bob behaved more like a coach than a boss. He visibly stepped back at times while still in office, allowing Greg to be in the spotlight and to make key decisions. Greg, to his credit, received Bob's counsel adeptly, translating what Bob offered in a way that worked for him, deciding what to accept and what to reject, but all the while behaving respectfully toward his mentor. The transition was not easy for either of them. There were awkward moments, and meetings at which employees seemed confused about who was the definitive decision maker. But when the CEO title passed to Greg, he was far more prepared than he would have been without Bob's coaching.

Not every outgoing chief executive has the personality or the ability to excel in this role without some help. And of course, if the outgoing CEO leaves abruptly, someone else must step in to coach or mentor the new leader.

The Role of the CHRO

Although the board is accountable for CEO succession, and an outgoing CEO should direct the process, someone needs to attend to the day-to-day details. That person should be the company's chief human resources officer. CHROs should be deeply involved in all aspects of succession (they often choose and manage the relationship with executive recruiters, for instance), and will thus have an advantage in organizing the transition. They usually interact with outside candidates earlier than anyone else in the company does.

CHROs should aim not only to coordinate a new leader's transition into the company, but also to become her primary counsel on people, politics, and culture. In this regard they should think of themselves as communicators, interpreters, and sounding boards. The new CEO will find it easy to obtain strategic, operational, and financial data while getting up to speed, but will need someone to explain other executives' personal backstories and interrelationships and why and how some of the company's more idiosyncratic practices evolved. Ideally, a CHRO can also offer candid feedback on how the new leader's early words and actions are perceived in the organization. If the new leader begins in the number two role, the CHRO is also in the best position to observe the developing relationship between her and the incumbent CEO and to advise both on navigating it. If the new leader encounters a problem during the transition, the CHRO should be the first to receive a call.

This work shouldn't wait until the new leader actually joins the organization. When a large retail company recruited an outsider to succeed the CEO, the company's CHRO called him the next day and explained that although they'd spent time together during the search process, he wanted a meeting to discuss an onboarding plan and the company's political structure. The CHRO traveled to the new CEO's distant city, and they spent hours talking about the challenges of transition. The new leader found it invaluable. "Once I'd accepted the job, all my thoughts were on how to leave [my current company]," and the conversation with the CHRO "focused my attention on what was ahead," he says. "There was a lot I didn't know, and the onboarding plan he went over was a good start." The CHRO reflects on the conversation: "Talking to him on his turf was important, and I wanted it to be informal and away from our offices." The two even spent time considering how the new CEO would inform his current boss and ease his departure, because the CHRO had a lot of experience with resignations. "He really appreciated it—it was a good icebreaker, and I think he got a sense of how I would be of help to him," the CHRO says. Reaching out positioned him to evolve into the new CEO's key counselor.

Unfortunately, not every company has a CHRO who's up to this task. Many HR department heads lack the skills for it or haven't earned enough stature with the CEO or the board to be entrusted with this duty. And some don't aspire to or see the potential for a role as influential as the CFO's or the CMO's. In such a case, the CEO should upgrade the position well before a succession takes place, and the board should be involved in specifying the expectations for the CHRO. An adept CHRO will be the company's go-to resource on topics of culture and talent and will have developed the interpersonal and political skills necessary to be listened to by peers and the CEO.

The Role of the Board

For directors, an important question during a CEO transition is how much distance they should keep. Directors aren't at a company full-time and thus see managers in action only periodically. They cannot and should not micromanage—but there is danger in being too remote. Directors often want to give a new CEO room as an expression of confidence, but this respectful gesture can keep them out of touch. And the new CEO may perceive it as a lack of interest or a message to sink or swim alone. The best boards strike a fine balance between being uninvolved and overinvolved.

When boards fail to find that balance, they're usually too distant. Incoming CEOs routinely report that they don't get enough transition support from directors—or that it doesn't last as long as they might wish. According to a 2012 study conducted by RHR International of 23 major CEO transitions, 57% of CEOs promoted from inside and 83% hired from outside said their boards were "less involved" than they should have been.

Clear expectations are among the most crucial things directors can provide. What kind of between-meetings communication do they expect? Do they prefer to weigh in or vote on fully formed, deeply researched plans and proposals, or do they want to have a hand in guiding nascent strategic ideas? One way to start the conversation is for the nonexecutive chair or the lead director to ask the new CEO to prepare answers to three questions: (1) What information do you need from the board to be able to do the best job you can? (2) What behavior on the board's part would best enable us to have a trusting relationship at board meetings, between them, and in one-on-one conversations? (3) From your experience during the search process and in your first meeting or two as CEO, what one thing about how the board operates would you change to help make our relationship all it must be?

Directors must realize that a CEO's relationship with the board as a whole is really a collection of relationships with individual directors. Experienced business leaders like Mark Thompson, who served as the CEO of two British media companies before becoming the chief executive of The New York Times Company in 2012, understand the importance of cultivating individual relationships with directors. When Thompson arrived at the Times Company, he devoted significant energy to doing just that. (See the sidebar "Inside One CEO's Transition.") Building those relationships may not come naturally or seem like a priority to first-time CEOs, however. If that's the case, directors should take the initiative, and the CHRO should help.

For a board, a CEO succession is a critical moment in the life of the company—a time when the directors should expect to be meeting, talking, and contributing more than they ordinarily do, much as they would during a merger or an acquisition. Though a CEO succession may require fewer emergency meetings, directors should treat it as an all-hands-on-deck period.

Most new leaders fail not because their financial or operational abilities are inadequate but because their style or political skills render them unprepared to manage the organization's culture. Helping new leaders understand that culture and improve their "soft skills" to successfully navigate it may be the best way to increase their chances of success.

An energetic and resourceful leader with intuition, perception, and strong interpersonal skills can certainly succeed on her own—but not without expending more time and energy than would be required in an organized transition process. As one CEO puts it, "My onboarding experience was just not helpful on the things I most needed. It wasn't horrible or even difficult—it was just sort of useless. I figured out on my own what I needed, but it could have been a lot easier and happened a lot faster."

Even when a company takes the comprehensive approach to succession suggested here, it's important to recognize that the formal transfer of title is not the end of the process. The new leader cannot be considered truly embedded until he wins the loyalty of the organization's most influential managers. That is the culmination of succession, and it may not occur until months after the formal handoff of power. It is signified not by an event but by behavior. Former Xerox CEO Anne Mulcahy describes observing such a moment in a meeting after the title had passed to her chosen successor, Ursula Burns: "Everyone was looking at her rather than me—the whole team's attention had just shifted, without a lot of drama. That's the way it should be."

And that's one sign of a successfully executed transition process.

Originally published in December 2016. Reprint R1612D

Inside One CEO's Transition

by Daniel McGinn

Mark Thompson calls it the "golden period"—the time between when a company's new CEO is announced and when he or she officially starts the job.

Thompson, who left the BBC to become CEO of The New York Times Company in 2012, had an unusually long golden period: Owing to the London Olympics and a commitment to lecture at Oxford, he waited three months before beginning work. The interval gave Thompson time to prepare and reflect—and it also allowed the Times Company to craft a two-week agenda of all-day meetings in the month before his arrival, which James Citrin, of Spencer Stuart, who led Thompson's hiring, calls the most comprehensive CEO onboarding program he's ever seen.

That thoroughness was driven in part by Thompson's unusual background. Although he'd led two large British media companies, he'd never worked at a U.S. company or in newspapers, and he was the Times Company's first external CEO in more than a century. In a 75-minute conversation with HBR's Daniel McGinn, Thompson reflected on the activities that were most helpful as he transitioned into the role. The highlights:

A successful transition starts during the interviews

Every job candidate asks questions to learn more about the company, but Thompson, who began his career as a TV journalist, dug deep, calling friends at the Times Company and competing organizations and asking, What is it like to work there? Does the organization really want to change? And if so, does the culture allow change to happen?

"You never get a complete answer to that," Thompson says. "You have to flip to instinct. But I felt that many people—and collectively, the board—were really aware of the need to change." (The board had fired Janet Robinson, the prior CEO, in December 2011.)

Demeanor during onboarding is crucial
Thompson attended 29 sessions led by dozens of Times Company executives, on topics ranging from overall strategy and finances to travel-and-expense policies and the pension plan. He listened and spoke carefully. "Everyone is watching the whole time—it's a fishbowl," he says. "They're looking to understand who you are and what your values are. Do you listen to what they say? Are you indecisive? Are you impulsive? It's all done in a very friendly way, but you're on show. How you respond to the PowerPoint presentations is really important. . . . You're not just absorbing stuff."

A good executive assistant can be a cultural translator
Thompson could have brought over his existing EA from the BBC. Instead he said that he "wanted an executive assistant who was the opposite of me—someone who was a deeply experienced Times person, who really understood the way the company worked and knew everyone," he says. The result: Mary Ellen LaManna, a 33 year company veteran. "Mary Ellen has been one of the most important people in the whole process," Thompson says. "She could really read the cultural issues in a way that I was blind to."

Participate in early decisions
Even before his official start date, Thompson began offering guidance on matters that needed immediate action. He interviewed candidates and helped lead the hiring of an SVP for video, a key growth area. He weighed in on (and supported) the board's nascent plans to sell the *Boston Globe* and the company's stake in About.com. When executive editor Jill Abramson and chairman Arthur Sulzberger Jr. were debating whether to publish investigative reporting on financial improprieties by top Chinese officials—a story likely to create business problems in China—they brought Thompson into

the discussion. "They asked, 'Do you think we should run it?'" he recalls. "It was a very early test. The answer, of course, was yes."

Get out of the office

Thompson visited the company's London and Paris offices and then, in his first weeks on the job, Abramson invited him to join her on a three-day swing through Silicon Valley, meeting with Tim Cook and Sheryl Sandberg, among others. The European visits gave him perspective, and the California trip helped him forge a relationship with Abramson in a company whose "church-state" divide gives the newsroom great power. "There's a real risk that the new CEO will spend the first six months in the C-suite, locked in rooms with the finance and strategy teams," he says. "That is part of what you do, but it's useful to get a sense of what it feels like away from headquarters."

Meet, greet, and eat

Once he'd taken charge, Thompson set out to meet the company's top 100 executives. Most days, he entertained small groups at in-office breakfasts and lunches. "Night after night, I'd take one person out for a drink and then have dinner with somebody else," he says. He avoided the temptation to assess talents and ability immediately and approached the task partly as a politician. "As a CEO, you need a network," he says. "You can't change organizations by e-mail edict, so you're trying to find parts of the organization that will help you drive change." He also met with individual board members in his early months.

Find the balance between impulsive and slow moving

Perhaps the trickiest piece of the transition for an outside CEO is appearing sure-footed from day one without overstepping. Thompson says, "Most people expect you to start telling them what you want them to do on your first morning. That's not reasonable or possible. But it helps if you've already met them and have begun understanding the world from their point of view. . . . The temptation is to shoot from the hip, to start forming snap judgments and barking out orders. If you don't do any of that, it's probably a problem. But the other extreme is to go into listening mode, where you can look very passive. So you're trying to find a spot on the landscape somewhere between those two extremes." Thompson says that many new CEOs talk about a 100-day plan, but he thinks a longer transition is more realistic. "You have a year to prove you're the right person for the job," he says. "I think a CEO who's not working out after a year is probably not going to work out."

Originally published in December 2016. Reprint R1612D

Comp Targets
That Work

by Radhakrishnan Gopalan, John Horn,
and Todd Milbourn

SETTING EXECUTIVE PERFORMANCE targets is one of the main responsibilities of any board of directors. Unfortunately, it's a task boards struggle with. From 2006 to 2014 nearly all of the 1,000 largest U.S. firms by market cap completely changed the metrics in their CEOs' pay-for-performance contracts at least once, and almost 60% changed them more than once. In some cases, of course, the revisions reflected shifts in strategic imperatives, but in many others they were attempts to fix problems that the metrics themselves had created.

The troubles associated with executive performance targets are well known. Most often they encourage short-termism. Cutting research and development to increase quarterly profitability or earnings per share, for instance, may compromise an organization's ability to introduce innovative products and services. Managers can also game the metrics—by, say, lowballing budgets and forecasts to set themselves easily achievable goals. And some executives manipulate performance numbers by accelerating revenue recognition or postponing discretionary expenditures.

What companies need, then, is an incentive structure that makes it easier to meet targets by creating actual value than by gaming the system. New research, in which two of us participated, points the way. (See the sidebar "About the Research.") The study, which analyzed data from the proxy statements of more than 900 large U.S. firms over 15 years, examined the link between the behavior of executives and company performance. We have drawn on its findings to identify four principles for designing incentive packages that encourage managers to deliver real, sustainable value.

Principle 1: Use Multiple Metrics

Many firms like to set simple targets for their executives and so assess performance against a single metric that they believe will capture a multitude of behaviors. The logic goes like this: If a CEO has only one metric to focus on, every decision will enhance it, so all you need to do is pick the one that will deliver the results you want. We find that many companies are deeply wedded to this thinking. When companies change a CEO's performance criteria, 40% of the time they simply choose another single metric.

But even metrics that encompass a broad range of activities can produce dysfunction when used alone. Consider EPS targets, which are very popular. If a strategic choice hurts revenue growth or delays new product launches but nevertheless improves EPS, then a CEO who has an EPS target will always be tempted to make that choice to increase his or her chances of earning a payout.

This problem goes away if you set multiple targets, such as EPS *and* revenue growth *and* new product introductions *and* R&D investment level (say, as a percentage of sales). It's very hard to game multiple interconnected targets simultaneously, and it becomes more difficult as the number of targets rises. Senior executives just don't have the time to do it. This was, in fact, what our data showed: Executives who had to achieve multiple goals to receive their bonuses were just as likely to miss a given target as they were to exceed it. Statistically, this is what you'd expect to see if no manipulation has taken place. In contrast, it is highly unlikely statistically that executives will just overperform most of the time. Such results are an indication that they are actively managing to their targets.

Idea In Brief

The Problem

Companies struggle to create executive comp packages that deliver desired performance.

Why It Happens

Performance targets are often easy to game. Managers can cut or postpone long-term investments to produce higher earnings today and can manipulate which expenses and revenues get recognized when.

The Solution

Comp committees should follow these four principles:

- Use multiple metrics.
- Increase payouts at a constant rate and adjust for risk.
- Reward performance relative to competitors.
- Include nonfinancial targets.

It's important to include a purely revenue-based target in the basket because that's harder to fudge than a profit target. It's easier to bridge a 10% profit shortfall than to bridge a 10% revenue shortfall by manipulating your sales. Let's say your revenue is $100 million and your total costs (assume they're fixed, for simplicity) are $90 million. A 10% profit shortfall would be $1 million, so you would have to find only an additional 1% of sales to close the gap. On the other hand, to meet a 10% sales shortfall, you'd have to come up with an extra $10 million.

It's also easier for senior executives to control costs than to control revenue. Consumer reaction to price cuts (or increases) is inherently uncertain and may take time to become apparent. But cost reductions often can be calibrated with enough precision to ensure that earnings (and EPS) meet the desired targets. This is especially true for the costs that senior executives most often focus on when adjusting to make EPS numbers: R&D and sales, general, and administrative expenses.

When you set multiple targets, make sure they aren't too closely correlated. Don't choose both earnings and EPS as key metrics, for example, because it will be as easy for the CEO to hit both targets as it would if she had to clear only an EPS hurdle. A better combination would be cash-flow growth and EPS, or revenue growth and earnings.

There is no magic number of targets to choose. Ultimately, it comes down to which metrics reflect the corporation's strategic objectives. A good rule of thumb, however, is to aim for three to five, because using just two could still create opportunities to manage to the targets while more than five can create confusion about where the organization should focus.

Principle 2: Increase Payouts at a Constant Rate, Adjusting for Risk

In most companies payouts for performance don't increase at a steady rate. Typically, executives don't receive one until some minimum threshold has been crossed; then their rewards rise steeply until a target is reached, after which the rewards tend to increase at a lower rate. Consider the incentive plan that one large U.S. technology company spelled out for its CEO in its 2017 proxy statement. The minimum threshold for the CEO was operating income of $295 million; at that point he'd receive 50% of his payout. His incentives rose sharply until operating income hit $328 million, at which point he'd receive 100% of the payout. Beyond that target, the payout for improved performance grew much more slowly. (See the exhibit "The hidden disincentives in performance plans.")

This type of compensation structure encourages performance gaming. There is less incentive for a CEO to push beyond the target, since additional performance improvement doesn't have the same incremental impact on his or her bonus. The data seems to bear this out: At companies where payout rates tapered off beyond a given target, CEOs tended to deliver results at or just above the target and seldom much beyond it.

For this reason we recommend that boards increase payouts at a constant rate relative to performance. When companies do this, actual results are less likely to bunch around the target. Of course, you don't want to encourage senior executives to take excessive risks to achieve higher and higher payouts, which means payouts should be capped at some maximum performance level. But you should be very explicit about why you are setting that cutoff point.

The hidden disincentives in performance plans

The bonus payout rates for the CEO of one high-tech company, depicted below, are typical of many companies. There's a minimum threshold the CEO has to hit to receive any payout and an overall target. From the threshold to the overall target, payouts rise at a steep rate; after that they taper off. Research shows that such setups may dampen performance at the high end: Managers tend not to exceed their targets by any significant amount.

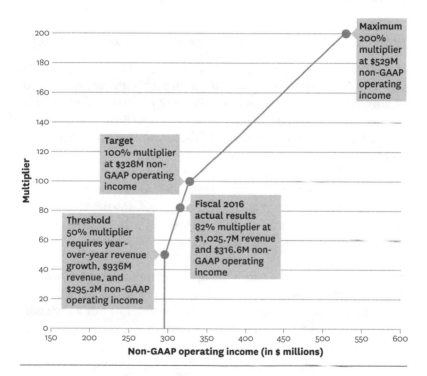

The board must also ensure that payout rates reflect the riskiness of a given target. Targets for EPS and return on equity, for example, can be achieved by increasing leverage at the company—perhaps to repurchase shares. To counter this, a board should adjust payouts on these metrics downward if the firm's capital structure becomes weaker or other risk factors increase during the performance period. The overall compensation plan, as well as the underlying strategy that it mirrors, must reflect the risk the company is willing to accept.

For example, a bank CEO's return-on-equity targets should be calibrated to the level of capital the bank maintains. Achieving a 10% ROE with a 12% capital ratio may be easier than achieving it with a 15% capital ratio, so the targets should progressively increase as the capital ratio falls.

Principle 3: Reward Performance Relative to Competitors

Most compensation packages set absolute goals, meaning that the CEO must hit a specific number to receive a bonus. In fact, the use of absolute goals has become increasingly pervasive over the past decade. In 2006 the payouts of 82% of CEOs and 89% of all top executives were pegged to them; by 2014 those numbers had risen to 93% and 98%, respectively.

It's certainly an easy approach. The board can just use analysts' forecasts to determine a goal, and the CEO gets a clear number to measure progress against. If you're feeling bold, the next time you're in a senior executive's office, ask whether his or her computer has a ticker active on it that tracks the company's stock price.

But absolute goals don't necessarily lead firms to reward performance. Say the board decides the appropriate target is 2% revenue growth. With an absolute metric, it would reward a CEO who grew revenue 2% while the sector overall grew 7%, but not a CEO who grew revenue 1.5% while the sector shrank 3%—even though the latter CEO did a better job.

By switching to relative targets, boards can avoid that kind of problem completely. Relative targets also make gaming far harder because the performance of competitors isn't known until they release results, which often happens weeks or months after the end of the performance period. Senior executives can't go back and manipulate numbers at that point. The best way to beat the competition, then, is to continually strive to improve the corporation's performance. The research confirms this: When CEOs had relative targets, company performance was either slightly greater than or slightly less than the relative target with equal likelihood, which is what you would expect in the absence of gaming.

Absolute targets let managers stay in their comfort zones, focusing on things they can more easily control, like R&D spending, SG&A spending, or landing a large contract. They have no incentive to look beyond that. Relative metrics, by contrast, encourage an outward focus: To outdo competitors, executives must also study them closely and find ways to create differentiated positions. Although there's a risk that the focus on rivals will cause some companies to rely too much on benchmarking, this will be balanced by the fact that at least one of them will always be innovating. And if the CEO wants to hit the relative targets in her contract, she can't merely copy those innovations—she'll have to create a distinctive advantage.

In setting relative targets, you need to think carefully about which competitors to follow. This comparison group should also be based on the firm's strategy. If the company is a major player in a mature industry, it will want to use its large competitors as the primary benchmarks. If the corporation is expanding into a new area as the core of its strategy, it should benchmark against smaller, newer rivals in that sector. The sweet spot will be more than one or two (which makes it too easy for the CEO to benchmark against others) and fewer than 10 (since the competitors' performance will have to be aggregated into one number for comparison).

Of course, the exact number of benchmarked competitors will depend on how many publicly owned companies are in the industry, and it's OK to pick bigger or smaller companies, provided you adjust the relevant benchmarks to account for differences with your corporation. For example, if you're a small player going up against a large conglomerate, you can use the results in the specific areas in which you compete with it as your benchmarks (if its results are broken out that granularly) or estimate what portion of its overall performance is accounted for by the division you compete with.

Principle 4: Include Nonfinancial Targets

Our final recommendation is to incorporate targets that are not directly related to sales and profits in any CEO performance contract. Although the research we base this article on didn't explicitly measure the effects of nonfinancial targets, it's clear that many of them are hard to game. To begin with, it often takes a significant amount of time for the results of decisions related to them to become apparent. Investments in employee training, for example, may not translate into employee productivity for a while. Additionally, many nonfinancial metrics, such as brand, reputation, and sustainability rankings, are set by outside agencies and so are hard for managers to manipulate.

What measures should you consider? Metrics like customer and employee satisfaction levels (as determined by broad-based surveys) are valuable because they provide leading indications about the long-term viability of an organization's strategy. If customers and employees aren't responding to the core value propositions the company is offering them, it will be hard to sustain revenue growth and profits or create an engaged workforce. Alaska Air Group, for example, has rated its CEOs on customer satisfaction, while Campbell Soup has included employee engagement in its CEO metrics. Visa ties executives' individual performance to "deep partnerships" and being "the employer of choice."

In our view it's important for every board to consider including a metric on how much a CEO respects and embodies the corporation's values. If top executives are not living up to these, it's quite possible the rest of the organization will follow, which could have disastrous effects on performance.

Probably the best way to assess adherence to values is through 360-degree feedback from peers, direct reports, board members, key customers, external partners, and other company stakeholders. ScottsMiracle-Gro applies to its executives' performance payouts a personal multiplier based on "a subjective assessment of effective leadership qualities such as team development, embodiment of the company's culture, and personal development and growth," according to its 2017 proxy statement.

About the Research

This article draws heavily on research by Benjamin Bennett, J. Carr Bettis, Radhakrishnan Gopalan, and Todd Milbourn that appeared in the May 2017 issue of the *Journal of Financial Economics*.

The study analyzed data from the proxy statements of the 750 largest U.S. firms (by market cap) from 1998 to 2012. Specifically, it looked at the performance targets CEOs had to reach to earn cash bonuses and grants of stock and options. The sample ultimately included 5,810 grants made by 974 firms. The authors calculated the difference between actual financial performance (in areas such as EPS, profitability, and sales) and the target level set for each metric in the individual CEO's performance incentive contract.

If targets are set reasonably and CEOs don't manipulate performance, they are statistically as likely to just beat a target as to just miss it (say, by a penny in either direction). But the study found that it was more likely for CEOs to just meet or slightly exceed a target than to slightly miss it, which suggests that executives are actively managing to their goals.

The authors also investigated differences across the design of pay-for-performance packages to explore the situations in which there was less managing to targets. Their findings in this area informed the recommendations of this article.

Finally, nonfinancial metrics on environmental, social, and governance performance are top of mind for many boards. In many corporations there is a strong link between short-term ESG goals and long-term financial performance. A reputation as an environmental steward, for example, may improve customer loyalty and enable premium pricing. In such situations tying part of compensation to ESG metrics is a great way to get the CEO to focus on the long term. But compensation committees should be alert to the risk that CEOs may massage ESG metrics to surpass their targets so that they can justify receiving a bonus if faced with a shortfall in current financial performance.

Creating a compensation package that adheres to the four guiding principles is not easy for a board. Directors need to debate multiple metrics (financial and nonfinancial alike), align them with the company's strategy and values, calibrate them with the risk appetite of the firm, and select an appropriate peer group to use as benchmarks. But this is ultimately what a board is there to do. If it uses executive compensation packages as a way to reinforce the company's competitive strategy and manage its risks, so much the better. Not only will it be more effective at communicating the strategy and rationale for top management pay with shareholders but it will also ensure that senior managers execute against the right objectives. Remember: Executives will do their best to hit whatever goals are set. So set targets that work for the corporation.

Originally published in September–October 2017. Reprint R1705H

The Case Against Long-Term Incentive Plans

Alexander Pepper spent 27 years at a large accounting firm helping client companies devise ways to compensate CEOs and other senior executives. Starting in the early 1990s, pay packages have typically included long-term equity incentive plans aimed at aligning managers' and shareholders' interests. But over time Pepper grew disillusioned. "I began to realize that the people we were putting the packages in place for didn't necessarily like them very much, and the plans didn't do what they were intended to," he says. In the early 2000s Pepper went back to school, eventually earning a DBA; he teaches at the London School of Economics. Today he researches why pay-for-performance plans don't work. "I was part of the system that I've subsequently come to say is not very effective," he says.

Since 2013 Pepper has published four academic studies based on in-depth surveys with 756 senior executives across 40 countries. He sought to measure how well the executives understand and value the components of their pay plans and how their pay affects their behavior. Although compensation practices differ dramatically from country to country—CEOs in the U.S. earn far more than their counterparts elsewhere, for instance—Pepper finds that regardless of region, executives have the same general misperceptions about pay. He identifies four reasons why pay-for-performance incentives don't work as well as proponents expected.

Executives are more risk-averse than financial theory suggests

Would you rather have a 50% chance of getting a $90,000 bonus, or a guaranteed payout of $41,250? In theory, the rational choice is the risky payout, since its "expected value" is $45,000, but 63% of executives chose the sure thing—and when asked similar questions involving stock option payouts, they consistently showed a preference for less risky choices. Someone who's risk-averse assigns less value to dicey propositions, which suggests that executives see the at-risk portions of pay packages as less valuable than economic theory would predict. In interviews they attribute this attitude partly to how "extraordinarily complex" and even "arbitrary" equity plans are. Pepper says that if people view something as not worth very much, more of that thing is needed to make it meaningful—and this dynamic inflates the value of pay plans.

Executives discount heavily for time

Would you rather get a $1 payout today or a $2 payout in a year? The rational choice is to wait, because you'll earn a 100% return during the interval, but behavioral economists have found that many people choose the early payout—a phenomenon called "hyperbolic discounting." Pepper's studies show that it applies to executives' thinking about pay: A long-term incentive package that may be worth a lot in three or four years is valued very little today. (His data suggests that executives discount distant payouts at the remarkable rate of 30% a year—about five times the discount economic theory suggests.) One executive in the study summed up the situation this way: "Companies are paying people in a currency they don't value."

Executives care more about relative pay

Consider a simple question: Would you rather earn $50,000 or $100,000? Now consider the same question with some added context: Would you rather earn $50,000 in a society where the median income is $30,000, or $100,000 in a society where the median income is $125,000? Assuming that prices are the same in both settings, you should choose $100,000—it lets you buy more, regardless of whether it's more or less than what other people make. But economists have long known that people are highly sensitive to relative earnings and prefer to outearn others even if it means a lower absolute income. Pepper's research shows that this holds for executive compensation. The executives surveyed were less concerned with absolute earnings and more focused on (and motivated by) how they were paid in relation to their peers, both inside the company and at rival firms. Fully 46% indicated that they would prefer a lower pay package if it was higher than those of counterparts. One said, "The only way I really think about compensation is, 'Do I feel fairly compensated relative to my peers?'" If everyone asks that question, the resulting arms-race mentality drives pay packages higher.

Pay packages undervalue intrinsic motivation

People work for all sorts of reasons, but executive pay packages tend to discount nonmonetary motivations. Pepper's research shows that achievement, status, power, and teamwork are all important incentives; in answering survey questions, executives made it clear that extra-large pay packages don't necessarily create stronger incentives. "I do not believe, nor have I ever observed, that $100 million motivates people more than $10 million or $1 million," said one company chairman. Executives said they would willingly reduce their pay packages by an average of 28% in exchange for a job that was better in other respects.

How should companies use these findings? Given that executives dramatically undervalue long-term incentive pay, Pepper believes that companies should eliminate that component and increase others. "My research suggests, somewhat perversely, that companies would be better off paying larger salaries and using annual cash bonuses to incentivize desired actions and behaviors," he says. Additionally, they should require leaders to invest those bonuses in company stock (or should pay the bonuses in the form of restricted stock) until a certain share of leaders' net worth, or some multiple of their annual salary, is invested. As long as executives hold substantial equity, Pepper says, their interests will be aligned with those of shareholders—and this arrangement would achieve that aim without the confusion and inefficiencies of long-term incentive plans. Some companies, including Berkshire Hathaway, already have plans structured along these lines.

Pepper and other observers recognize that companies looking to implement such changes will face headwinds. In the United States, for instance, salaries above $1 million are not tax deductible, and in most countries the notion of pay for performance is so ingrained that big salary increases could draw criticism. However, Pepper says that like fashion, executive pay tends to go through cycles, and he believes that the long-term incentives in vogue for the past quarter century may soon fall out of favor. "My argument is that pay for performance makes the problem worse, not better," he says. "You can pay executives considerably less in total—but do it in a different way."

About the Research

Pepper's studies, conducted with the University of Bath's Julie Gore, are described in his book *The Economic Psychology of Incentives: New Design Principles for Executive Pay* (Palgrave Macmillan, 2015).

Originally published in October 2016. Reprint F1610A

Sustainability in the Boardroom

by Lynn S. Paine

A BOARD MEMBER WAS EXCHANGING a few words with the CEO of a fast-growing athletic apparel maker before the annual shareholders' meeting when the two caught sight of a group of labor activists at the back of the hall. The group was known for protesting labor conditions in the Asian contract factories where the company's products were made. The CEO turned to the director and, without prior warning, said that he planned to ask her to take charge of the meeting if any disruption occurred. When the activists marched to the front of the auditorium partway through the meeting, that's exactly what he did.

Although corporate directors are often faced with difficult questions about the conduct of the companies they serve, rarely are they confronted in such a public fashion. But that's what happened to Jill Ker Conway at Nike's 1996 annual meeting. A former president of Smith College and a self-proclaimed jock, Conway had been recruited to Nike's board by the chairman and then-CEO, Phil Knight, in 1987 for her expertise on women's issues and her understanding of the student perspective.

Fortunately, Conway was not taken wholly unawares when Knight called on her to chair the proceedings. A few months earlier she had told him that she expected labor issues in the contract factories to come up at the meeting and felt that at least one director should be able to speak about them firsthand. During that conversation she had offered to visit some of Nike's contract factories in Southeast Asia as part of a trip she was about to take to her native Australia. With Knight's blessing, she had made the first in what would become an extensive series of visits over the next few years. So she was well equipped to preside when a heated exchange broke out between the labor group's leader and the assembled shareholders and, later, to advise on a formal research effort that would shape many of Nike's early corporate responsibility initiatives.

Much has been written about Nike's extensive corporate responsibility efforts and how they have transformed the company from an organization whose name was synonymous (as Phil Knight said in 1998) with "slave wages, forced overtime, and arbitrary abuse" to a pioneer in using social and environmental issues as catalysts for innovation. Far less attention has been paid to the board's role in these efforts or to Nike's creation of a board-level corporate responsibility committee to institutionalize the company's commitment to responsible performance.

That's not surprising. Those engaged in the mainstream corporate governance discussion have been largely silent on the subject of the board's role in overseeing corporate responsibility and sustainability. Why that's so is not entirely clear, especially with the increasing pressures on (and opportunities for) companies to help address serious economic, social, and environmental problems around the globe. It may result in part from the intense focus over the past decade on financial reporting, executive compensation, and board leadership in the wake of the Sarbanes-Oxley Act, the 2008 financial crisis, and the Dodd-Frank Act. Although that focus has been mainly to the good, one unfortunate side effect has been the relative neglect of other aspects of governance.

In view of growing concern about business and sustainability, and given the importance of corporate responsibility for ongoing value creation, directors should be asking whether their board's oversight in those areas is sufficient. Recent surveys suggest that no more than 10% of U.S. public company boards have a committee dedicated solely to corporate responsibility or sustainability. Nike's experience indicates that such a committee could be a useful addition to many

Idea in Brief

The Problem

Although more and more companies recognize the importance of corporate responsibility and sustainability to their long-term success, these issues get short shrift in most boardrooms.

The Solution

To address the risks and opportunities arising from problems such as climate change, water pollution, corruption, and uneven access to wealth, health, and education, Nike's board created a dedicated corporate responsibility committee in 2001.

The Results

Nike's experience suggests that such a committee could be useful to many companies' boards in at least five ways: as a source of knowledge and expertise, as a sounding board and constructive critic, as a driver of accountability, as a stimulus for innovation, and as a resource for the full board.

if not most boards in at least five ways: as a source of knowledge and expertise, as a sounding board and constructive critic, as a driver of accountability, as a stimulus for innovation, and as a resource for the full board. A look at how Nike's corporate responsibility committee has served each of these functions will show why.

A Source of Knowledge and Expertise

Chief executives often seek directors who have expertise and relationships that could help the company, but rarely with corporate responsibility or sustainability issues in mind. Yet domain-specific knowledge and relationships are as relevant for those areas as for any others.

When protests over labor practices abroad broke out on U.S. college campuses in the mid-1990s, Nike was fortunate to have in Conway a director with extensive knowledge of the student population and expertise in the societal effects of industrialization. That was not entirely by chance. Conway had been recruited as part of Knight's efforts to bring fresh thinking and experience to the boardroom at a time when the company was struggling to regain the momentum of its first decade. With the notable exception of one director who was an expert on innovation and creativity, the board had consisted mainly of friends and family of Nike's founding group.

As it happened, in adding Conway, the board got geographic, gender, experience, network, and knowledge diversity all at once. So when the activists took to the floor at the 1996 shareholders' meeting, Conway recognized the complexity of the situation. She knew that the protests would only escalate and that improving factory conditions would take time.

Conway is an authority on women's entry into the paid workforce in 19th-century Britain and the United States. Her knowledge of the impact of industrialization on the lives of women and girls made her an especially well-informed observer during her visits to factories in countries that were undergoing industrialization. After Nike hired Maria Eitel as its first vice president of corporate responsibility, in 1998, Conway and Eitel brokered a partnership with the International Youth Foundation to create a nonprofit that would study the largely young female workforce in the factories. Staffers of the nonprofit thus created—the Global Alliance for Workers and Communities—interviewed 67,000 workers in their native languages at off-site locations where the workers could speak fully and freely. Without Conway's ability to tap a global network of women's organizations and university faculty members, Nike would have found it difficult to gain access to those communities in view of the company's reputation at the time.

In 2001 Conway proposed the creation of a board-level corporate responsibility committee. She wanted to engage the board not just in the labor issues that were threatening Nike's reputation among its core consumers but also in a range of other topics that were not being raised to the board. Chief among them were health and environmental issues, which were beginning to command attention both inside and outside the company. Knight endorsed the idea and asked Conway to serve as chair. She accepted on the condition that Knight attend every meeting—her way of making sure that the committee would not be marginalized. "Everybody wanted to come before that committee," Conway recalls; people knew that doing so would put them squarely in front of Knight.

The close alignment between Conway's diverse talents and the corporate responsibility issues Nike faced in the 1990s may have been fortuitous, but boards need not leave the matter of fit to chance. Mapping out the company's principal responsibilities and identifying key issues the firm is likely to confront can reveal the areas of knowledge and experience that would be particularly valuable to have represented on the committee. Members should have an understanding of stakeholders' expectations and the company's governing standards, but imagination, openness to new ideas, and an interest in innovation are also crucial.

The expertise currently gathered in Nike's corporate responsibility committee, for instance, reflects both the company's perennial labor issues and its recent focus on sustainability and innovation. The group includes a university chancellor with a background in biological science and environmental education, a former university basketball coach, a chief executive in an industry whose lifeblood is innovation, a retired media company executive and university trustee, and a former trial lawyer with four decades of service on the Nike board.

A Sounding Board and Constructive Critic

A labor incident in the supply chain. A controversial disclosure. A shift in sustainability strategy. A change in organizational structure. A proposal to invest in a new environmental technology. The range of corporate responsibility issues that Nike (or any company) might face is complex and varied. By asking insightful questions, making suggestions, offering perspectives, raising counterpoints, and proposing alternatives, the committee enriches and challenges management's thinking.

Take what happened in 2009, when the committee was considering a thorny situation involving two subcontractors in Honduras who had closed their doors and dismissed 1,800 employees without notice and without paying the roughly $2 million in severance that

Setting Up a Board-Level Corporate Responsibility Committee

JILL KER CONWAY chaired the Nike board's committee from 2001 until her retirement from the board, in 2011. She recently spoke with Lynn Paine about how the committee was created and what makes it effective.

PAINE: In 2001 you proposed the creation of a board-level committee as a way to institutionalize Nike's commitment to corporate responsibility. Why did you think that was important?

CONWAY: I had worked on corporate responsibility issues when I was a director of IBM World Trade. They had many problems about introducing their technology into the developing world and making a lot of money out of it but not really responding to the needs of the society. So I had some experience of what those committees could do. I also felt that because people come and go, if you have a legitimate structure for managing these issues, they are much better dealt with—knowledge and understanding accumulate, better records are kept, and so on.

Why aren't such committees more common? Do you think a company's ownership structure has any bearing on this question? I ask because Nike has a controlling shareholder who was also a founder, and I wonder what effect, if any, that has had on the company's handling of these issues.

I'm absolutely certain it has had an effect. When we set up the Global Alliance to do our survey of workers, I trekked around the world trying to recruit other consumer products companies with the same kinds of supply chains to join us. The only ones that had any interest were those with significant family ownership. I don't think executives of a typical public corporation have that same feeling of moral responsibility that the principal founder or owner has.

Speaking more practically, do you have any suggestions for a director who believes the board needs to be more engaged with corporate responsibility issues but isn't sure how to make it happen?

Well, number one, the person has to be committed to the enterprise totally and not be a complainer. Second, I think they have to have some kind of intellectual framework into which they can fit what they are urging people to do. You can't just say, "It would be nice if we did things better for low-income countries and poor families." You have to really have some picture of what might be achieved by undertaking some major changes. And third, you can't be afraid to be criticized. You need a sense of humor and the ability to get people laughing so that they are relaxed when they're trying to talk about this subject rather than holding on to the edge of the table and worrying.

Are there particular skills or perspectives that should be represented on a corporate responsibility committee?

One thing that's very important is to have members who are deeply interested in innovation. You need people who are imaginative, open to new ideas, and capable of envisioning a different organization of things. Of course, you also have to have some core values. I'm a committed feminist, and I was bound to do the best I could to see that this major economic transformation didn't leave young women stranded just the way they'd always been.

What are some of the factors that make for an effective corporate responsibility committee?

It's very important to work with the finance committee and the financial analysts, because there's always a lot of loose talk about how much this or that is going to cost or whether it's going to have any yield. Another thing that is always persuasive and gets people nodding in agreement is the committee's sense that a lot of really bad mistakes are being avoided and a lot of fruitful opportunities are being created. It's also important to put people at ease when talking about difficult subjects. Sometimes you need to talk to people one-on-one and just take the time to find out what's on their mind or why they're troubled. When we were beginning, I went around and asked everybody what they thought this committee should do. We talked about the business model and what new ways of evolving it might come out of such a committee, and so on.

How does boardroom culture affect the corporate responsibility discussion?

One of the things I've been struck by is all my colleagues on the Nike board, whatever their political orientation, saying, "I have learned more on this board than from anything else I've done." I believe nobody thinks about board structures as a place where you really gain new knowledge and new insight, but I think my colleagues would all say that.

Where does that sense of learning come from?

It's how the board is run. You know, the board has dinner together every board meeting. And some unfortunate person is picked on by Phil to start

(continued)

Setting Up a Board-Level Corporate Responsibility Committee (*continued*)

the discussion of some important long- range subject. These are long discussion dinners, where people talk about what the original goal was for the company, how it has grown, what we are doing that's true to that dream, and so on. And in the board meeting, nobody is afraid of asking a question or looking silly—it's very open. Phil usually sits in the middle of the boardroom and is very quiet and just lets people start talking. The freedom with which people are encouraged to talk about things that they may not feel they know all that much about leads to a different kind of discourse. It sends people home saying, "That was really interesting at the board session. I've got to go look that up."

It sounds like a really fun board.
It is. It is. People just love it.

---

the employees were owed under local law. Nike had no legal responsibility for the severance payments and had stated publicly that it would not cover them. But pressure mounted from universities and student groups across the United States for Nike to make good on the subcontractors' obligations.

The discussion, led by Conway, was intense. The committee brainstormed ways to help the workers without setting a precedent for Nike's paying out whenever a subcontractor defaulted on obligations to its employees. After the meeting the management team decided to rethink Nike's position. The result was an innovative arrangement whereby the Honduran government made the severance payments while Nike created a $1.5 million workers' relief fund and provided support for vocational training and health coverage for the laid-off workers.

Even when committee discussions ultimately reinforce a direction that has been proposed, the process can highlight strengths and weaknesses in management's thinking and point to critical communication and execution challenges. That was the case in 2011 and 2012, when Nike was developing its next-generation sustainability targets. For nearly a decade the company had from time to time announced targets and reported progress in areas such as labor conditions in the contract factories, the use of environmentally preferred materials, and reducing greenhouse gas emissions, waste, and toxic substances in the supply chain—issues that by 2006 were being discussed under the mantle of "sustainability." By 2011 the previous targets had largely been achieved. The management team wanted to link the company's new sustainability targets more tightly with its growth strategy and day-today operations by providing specific sustainability goals for business and functional units across the organization.

That was a massive undertaking. For more than six months a dedicated team worked with managers and experts throughout the company to identify potential target areas and define measurable objectives for each. At various points the team advised the committee of its progress and shared its methodology, eventually floating preliminary proposals for targets. The committee had several responses. It questioned whether the targets were ambitious enough—and realistic enough. Some directors asked whether there were too many metrics and whether broader goals would be preferable to specific targets in certain areas. Others wanted to know more about what factors had been taken into account and how the pros and cons had been weighed. In the end, the committee's stress test did not change the team's approach. But the scrutiny lent assurance that the thinking was robust, and it provided a useful preview of likely reactions to the proposed targets from managers and others who had not yet been involved. And, of course, the prospect of review by a dedicated board-level committee gave the team an added incentive to proceed with rigor throughout the process.

The committee's value as a sounding board depends as much on its distinctive outlook as on the specific knowledge and experience that its members bring to the discussion. Four of the five members of Nike's committee are independent directors, which means that they combine a third-party perspective with the loyalty, care, and confidentiality required of fiduciaries. At once outsiders and insiders, they are uniquely positioned to be the constructive skeptics every good management team needs, especially when dealing with issues that affect the public interest.

A Driver of Accountability

One of the newly established committee's initial tasks was to oversee the publication of Nike's first stand-alone corporate responsibility report. The committee continues to oversee public reporting on corporate responsibility and sustainability, but it also fosters accountability through a range of other activities. It spends the first half of each regular two- hour meeting (held five times a year, in conjunction with the full board's regular meetings) reviewing the company's progress toward its sustainability targets along with the contract factories' performance against Nike's health, safety, environmental, and other standards. The factory discussions focus on trends in performance rather than on compliance audits (those are conducted by a group within the corporate audit function that reports to the CFO and to the audit committee of the board).

To assess and track performance, the committee relies on data generated by the management team using Nike's factory-rating system, which includes various measures of labor and environmental performance in addition to the traditional measures of product quality, cost, and delivery. At each meeting the committee examines current ratings, considers trends over time and across regions, addresses pressing issues, and tries to identify opportunities for improvement.

In conducting these oversight activities, the committee engages directly with key executives. True to Knight's 2001 pledge to Conway, either Knight or the current CEO, Mark Parker, attends each meeting. The executive in charge of corporate responsibility (initially Eitel, now Hannah Jones) has also worked closely with the committee since its inception. In 2009, as part of an effort to embed sustainability principles more deeply in the business, a second senior executive was added as a liaison to the committee: Eric Sprunk, at the time the vice president of merchandising and products and now the COO. This change at the board level coincided with changes at the corporate level, including the introduction of dual-reporting lines between the corporate responsibility group and key business functions such as finance, innovation, and supply chain, and an expansion of the corporate responsibility group's work from achieving day-to-day operational compliance to building a fundamentally more sustainable business model. The shift in orientation was reflected in the group's adoption of a new name—"sustainable business and innovation"—and the creation of the SB&I lab, an in-house group that includes members with private equity and venture capital expertise and is charged with seeking external technologies and partnerships to advance the sustainability agenda.

Perhaps the most potent way in which the committee fosters accountability is through regular meetings with executives and managers from different business and functional areas. The second hour of committee meetings is typically devoted to a particular strategy or activity of the SB&I group and a particular strategy or activity of a business unit or function. Under the format put in place in 2009, heads of the business units or functions typically appear before the committee at least once every 18 months to explain how their strategies align with SB&I strategies and how that alignment is reflected in their group's accountability metrics. CFO Don Blair says that the experience of presenting to the committee and having committee members sitting across the table asking questions "puts a little backbone into what the business leader is undertaking to do."

A Stimulus for Innovation

One surprising role of Nike's corporate responsibility committee is to provide support and encouragement for innovation, especially innovation aimed not just at improving operations incrementally but also at building a fundamentally more sustainable business model. For Nike that means a business model that can continue to deliver growth in the face of looming macro-environmental challenges such as resource scarcity, climate change, and demographic shifts, to name just a few.

When Conway and Eitel initiated the contract factory studies, they took a strategic approach to improving working conditions, recognizing that actors in addition to Nike would be crucial to continued success. Community groups, government authorities, and outside experts would have to be mobilized to tackle problems stemming as much from weaknesses in local institutions and infrastructure as from Nike's practices. And because many of the factories made products for other companies as well, it would be necessary to engage other industry players.

Accordingly, when asked by the top leadership team in 2001 whether Nike should disclose the results of the worker interview project, the committee said yes, hoping that would foster the broader engagement needed for widespread improvements in labor conditions. Similarly, in 2005, when Jones proposed disclosing the names and locations of Nike's contract factories—information that was typically treated as highly proprietary—the committee lent its support. Some feared that the move would put Nike at a disadvantage, enabling competitors to more easily poach its suppliers. But Jones reasoned that the benefits of disclosure would outweigh the risks. Transparency would let Nike's critics see factory conditions for themselves. It would also allow Nike to work with other companies that used the same suppliers in order to coordinate inspections, share costs, and adopt common standards, thus improving labor conditions across the industry.

In its early years, the committee spent much of its time providing advice and, in Conway's words, "putting out fires"—reacting to individual incidents, such as serious breaches of labor standards in the supply chain or major problems affecting health, safety, or the environment. As management began developing more-sophisticated systems to monitor factory compliance with Nike's code of conduct, the committee became more focused on overseeing those systems. Once it was clear that some of the individual incidents the systems identified were part of a larger pattern, the committee's work evolved again.

An 18-month-long task force formed by management in 2005 to study the recurring problem of excessive overtime found that the root cause lay not only in factory deficiencies but also in sudden changes Nike made to materials or volume requirements in response to fluctuations in demand. This insight had profound ramifications: Management and the committee realized that they had reached the limits of what monitoring could accomplish. Better policing would not resolve the labor issue; what was needed were innovative ways to make manufacturing processes inherently safer and more sustainable. As Jones put it, "You can either solve a workers' rights issue by monitoring every single factory 24 hours a day for whether they're wearing protective equipment, or you can innovate a new glue that removes all the toxics so that you don't have to have the personal protective equipment."

So today, although the committee remains engaged in monitoring, oversight, problem solving, and even firefighting on occasion, it spends considerable time advising on Nike's innovation efforts. For example, in 2012 it weighed in on a proposed strategic investment in DyeCoo Textile Systems, a small Netherlands-based start-up that had developed a waterless process for dyeing polyester using recycled CO_2 (hence the name DyeCoo). In addition to saving the 12 to 18 gallons of water per pound of fabric used in traditional dyeing methods, the new technology eliminates chemical discharges into the water supply. Moreover, not having to heat water for dyeing saves energy and cuts dyeing times in half—and a higher-quality product results. But the process was not yet cost-competitive with traditional methods. Management sought the committee's views on a proposal to take a minority stake in DyeCoo with the aim of helping the Dutch company develop and commercialize the technology for use in textile mills and dye houses in the global apparel supply chain. The committee supported the proposal, and Nike made the investment. In late 2013 a Nike contract manufacturer in Taiwan opened a facility that uses DyeCoo's technology.

The extent of the corporate responsibility committee's focus on innovation came as a surprise to the current chair, Phyllis Wise, when she joined the committee in 2009, shortly after being elected to the board. At the time, Wise was the interim president of the University of Washington, where she had overseen the creation of its College of the Environment. She expected that the committee would focus mainly on monitoring labor conditions in the contract factories—still a hot topic on university campuses. But she found that it also spent a great deal of time on innovation processes, product development, new materials, and other forward-looking initiatives. As the top leadership team pursues its quest for game-changing innovations that can drive sustainable growth and profitability, the committee is likely to become even more engaged in the innovation discussion.

A Resource for the Full Board

Perhaps the most important function of Nike's corporate responsibility committee is to serve as a custodian of the long view—a counterweight to the myopia that can result from the pressure of short-term objectives and the relentless flow of matters demanding immediate attention. Of the wide spectrum of topics that come before the committee, a significant number involve future conditions or parties who do not currently have a direct market relationship with the company but whose actions could have a powerful effect on its future health and functioning. This group includes factory workers in the supply chain and the millions of ordinary citizens affected by Nike's activities. It also extends to future generations of Nike managers, who may face shortages of critical resources; future generations of consumers and athletes who use Nike products; and beneficiaries of the company's community investment activities, who may one day become influential members or leaders of their communities and countries.

Many companies say that such issues are the responsibility of the full board, and that is certainly true. Yet how many boards actually take up these issues on a regular basis? The evidence suggests that the answer is very few. A review of the annual director surveys conducted by the National Association of Corporate Directors over the past decade indicates that corporate responsibility issues are consistently ranked at the bottom of some two dozen possible board priorities. Nike executives say that board-level discussions of labor issues in the supply chain gained traction only after the corporate responsibility committee was formed.

Creating a corporate responsibility committee does not absolve the full board of its obligation to oversee this aspect of the company's performance. But such a committee can help the board fulfill this obligation through its focus, expertise, and sustained attention. From focus and sustained attention come deeper understanding, better processes, and more-refined instincts. A regular report from the committee to the full board, comparable to reports from other standing committees, can help raise the board's level of understanding and ensure that critical issues receive the scrutiny they require.

Given the litany of economic, social, and environmental problems plaguing societies around the globe, issues of corporate responsibility and sustainability are likely to become ever more salient. Many companies will face difficult questions of resource allocation, and some may find their business models under attack. Strategically, companies will have to decide whether (and how) to go on the offense and invest in innovation or to bulk up on defense and strengthen their compliance and risk management functions—or both. Individual directors will increasingly be expected to speak to those issues. The time has come for business leaders, boards, and governance experts to start talking about the role of boards and board committees in addressing these questions and to consider whether a corporate responsibility committee should be part of the answer.

Originally published in July–August 2014. Reprint R1407G

About the Contributors

DOMINIC BARTON is the global managing partner of McKinsey & Company and a trustee of the Brookings Institution. He is coauthor of *Talent Wins: The New Playbook for Putting People First* (Harvard Business Review Press, 2018).

DEBORAH BELL is a researcher of organizational behavior whose work focuses on leadership, drivers of success, and organizational effectiveness and dynamics, especially at the board level.

JOSEPH L. BOWER is the Donald Kirk David Professor Emeritus at Harvard Business School and coauthor of the book *Capitalism at Risk: Rethinking the Role of Business* (Harvard Business Review Press, 2011).

RICHARD P. CHAIT is a professor at Harvard University's Graduate School of Education and coauthor of *Governance as Leadership: Reframing the Work of Nonprofit Boards* (John Wiley & Sons, 2005).

RAM CHARAN has been an adviser to the CEOs of some of the world's biggest corporations and their boards. He is a coauthor of *Talent Wins: The New Playbook for Putting People First* (Harvard Business Review Press, 2018).

DAN CIAMPA is a former CEO, an adviser to boards and chief executives, and the author of five books, including *Transitions at the Top: What Organizations Must Do to Make Sure New Leaders Succeed* (with David L. Dotlich, Wiley, 2015) and *Right from the Start: Taking Charge in a New Leadership Role* (with Michael Watkins, Harvard Business Review Press, 1999).

SARAH CLIFFE is an executive editor at the *Harvard Business Review*.

GEORGE DAVIS was formerly the Global CEO & Board Practice Leader at Egon Zehnder and is currently the executive vice president of MacAndrews & Forbes.

BARBARA HACKMAN FRANKLIN served as the 29th U.S. secretary of commerce and is the president and CEO of Barbara Franklin Enterprises, a consulting firm that advises American companies doing business in international markets.

RADHAKRISHNAN GOPALAN is a professor at the Olin Business School at Washington University in St. Louis.

BORIS GROYSBERG is the Richard P. Chapman Professor of Business Administration at Harvard Business School, faculty affiliate at the HBS Gender Initiative, and the coauthor, with Michael Slind, of *Talk, Inc: How Trusted Leaders Use Conversation to Power their Organizations* (Harvard Business Review Press, 2012).

LINDA A. HILL is the Wallace Brett Donham Professor of Business Administration at Harvard Business School. She is author of *Becoming a Manager: How New Managers Master the Challenges of Leadership* and coauthor of *Being the Boss: The 3 Imperatives for Becoming a Great Leader* and *Collective Genius: The Art and Practice of Leading Innovation*.

THOMAS P. HOLLAND is professor emeritus at the University of Georgia's School of Social Work.

JOHN HORN is a senior lecturer at the Olin Business School at Washington University in St. Louis.

STEFANIE K. JOHNSON is an associate professor of management and entrepreneurship at University of Colorado's Leeds School of Business and author of *Inclusify: The Power of Uniqueness and Belonging to Build Innovative Teams* (Harper Business, 2020).

ROBERT S. KAPLAN is a senior fellow and the Marvin Bower Professor of Leadership Development, emeritus, at Harvard Business School.

JAMES MANYIKA is the chairman of the McKinsey Global Institute (MGI), the business and economics research arm of McKinsey & Company.

DANIEL MCGINN is a senior editor at *Harvard Business Review*.

ANETTE MIKES is an assistant professor in the accounting and management unit at Harvard Business School.

TODD MILBOURN is a vice dean and the Hubert C. & Dorothy R. Moog Professor of Finance at the Olin Business School at Washington University in St. Louis.

DAVID A. NADLER was an American organizational theorist, consultant and business executive, known for his work with Michael L. Tushman on organizational design and organizational architecture. He was founding director of the consultancy firm Organization Research and Consultation, which became the Delta Consulting Group, Inc., and then Mercer Delta Consulting, LLC, where he served as chairman. He died in 2015.

LYNN S. PAINE is the John G. McLean Professor of Business Administration at Harvard Business School. She is a coauthor of *Capitalism at Risk: Rethinking the Role of Business* (Harvard Business Review Press, 2011).

DAVID PYOTT is a philanthropist and the former CEO of Allergan.

JEFFREY A. SONNENFELD is the senior associate dean for executive programs and the Lester Crown professor at the Yale School of Management. He is the founding CEO of Yale's Executive Leadership Institute.

BARBARA E. TAYLOR is a senior consultant at the Academic Search Consultation Service in Washington, D.C. and coauthor of *Governance as Leadership: Reframing the Work of Nonprofit Boards* (John Wiley & Sons, 2005).

SARAH KEOHANE WILLIAMSON is CEO of FCLT Global.

Index

Engage with HBR content the way you want, on any device.

With HBR's new subscription plans, you can access world-renowned **case studies** from Harvard Business School and receive **four free eBooks**. Download and customize prebuilt **slide decks and graphics** from our **Visual Library**. With HBR's archive, top 50 best-selling articles, and five new articles every day, HBR is more than just a magazine.

Subscribe Today
hbr.org/success

The most important management ideas all in one place.

We hope you enjoyed this book from *Harvard Business Review*. Now you can get even more with HBR's 10 Must Reads Boxed Set. From books on leadership and strategy to managing yourself and others, this 6-book collection delivers articles on the most essential business topics to help you succeed.

HBR's 10 Must Reads Series

The definitive collection of ideas and best practices on our most sought-after topics from the best minds in business.

- Change Management
- Collaboration
- Communication
- Emotional Intelligence
- Innovation
- Leadership
- Making Smart Decisions

- Managing Across Cultures
- Managing People
- Managing Yourself
- Strategic Marketing
- Strategy
- Teams
- The Essentials

hbr.org/mustreads

Buy for your team, clients, or event.
Visit hbr.org/bulksales for quantity discount rates.